Praise for *Dry Bones:*

Redeeming Your Past

"In *Dry Bones: Redeeming Your Past*, Kevin Goos graciously takes us on his journey from failure and shame to restoration. His transparency is refreshing and inspiring! Kevin shares with us, his God-given, biblical and doable tools so that we too can be restored from woundedness and possible bad choices from our past to help others. *Dry Bones* may trigger tears of joy if you're willing to face your past with God, accept God's forgiveness and learn to experience God's hope and grace for your restoration or for someone wounded. This is a must read!"

- Dr. Clarence Shuler, President/CEO of BLR: Building Lasting Relationships. Co-authored with Dr. Gary Chapman, *Choose Greatness*.

"Kevin and Barb's story is one I have been privileged to observe as a friend and a supervisor. They are real people who have faced great heartbreak and have truly come to understand how healing occurs. This account of their story and what they have learned is amazing and very helpful for real people who have found many of the church's glib answers to be insufficient. Read it with an open heart and God will use it to re-create your spirit in His great image."

- Rev. Wesley Smith. District Superintendent, Northwest District of the Wesleyan Church.

Dry Bones:

Redeeming Your Past

Kevin and Barb Goos

Published by KHARIS PUBLISHING, imprint of KHARIS MEDIA LLC.

Copyright © 2019 Kevin and Barb Goos

ISBN-13: 978-1-946277-48-0
ISBN-10: 1-946277-48-7

Library of Congress Control Number: 2019948944

All KHARIS PUBLISHING products are available at special quantity discounts for bulk purchase for sales, promotions, premiums, fund-raising, and educational needs. For details, contact:

Kharis Media LLC

Tel: 1-479-599-8657

support@kharispublishing.com

www.kharispublishing.com

CONTENTS

Introduction

As Ezekiel looked over the valley of dry bones, God asked him if these bones could live again. Recognizing he was being asked about something seemingly impossible, Ezekiel wisely answered, "Lord God, You know." God then showed him the answer. Bones became skeletons, skeletons became bodies, and bodies became people ready to come back to life. Restoration happened right before Ezekiel's eyes, to the point that an army was standing before him, only needing the breath of God to breathe life into them. When God breathed His life into them, what was dead was now alive. What was broken was now healed. What was mired in the past was now full of potential for the future. This vision was a picture of a future hope for Israel, and it was also a promise for people then as well as now. God promised to place His Spirit in those beyond hope and perform His great promises to them and for them.

This vision from Ezekiel 37 was spoken to provide that kind of hope for people who were suffering consequences because of sin and brokenness. This included sins committed against them and those done by them. They felt abandoned and stuck in their present circumstances. They voiced their despair and then God answered:

> *"Our bones are dry, our hope is lost, and we ourselves are cut off!" Therefore prophesy and say to them, "Thus says the Lord GOD: 'Behold, O My people, I will open your graves and cause you to come up from your graves, and bring you into the land of Israel. Then you shall know that I am the LORD, when I have opened your graves, O My people, and brought you up from your graves. I will put My Spirit in you, and you shall live, and I will place you in your own land. Then you shall know that I, the LORD, have spoken it and performed it,' says the LORD."*

—Ezekiel 37:11-14

"Our bones are dry. Our hope is lost." That is an accurate depiction on how many people feel in the deep places of their soul. The reasons why are vast and varied. It can be a person looking in the mirror at themselves with disappointment. A person could be looking at broken relationships with their marriage/children. There could be a sense of failure with their job/education prospects, their finances. It could be an overwhelming sense of helplessness as people look at their city/state/nation, or the condition of the world.

As people lose hope, they look back in the past and wonder what could have been. They look at the present and wonder if something can be done. They look at a bleak future and just might dare to imagine what could be if some things were different. People want to see the past redeemed. They want a meaningful life in the present and a true hope for the future. They don't want to be seemingly lifeless, surviving from day to day like dry bones needing a resurrection. In the midst of this angst and anguish, I am here to declare that dry bones can live again. The past can be redeemed, the present can be restored, and the future can be reclaimed. As we launch in this journey, we want you to know that anyone's dry bones can live again, and three words point the way.

Redeeming Your Past are the words guiding this book. It is the hope everyone can experience and the healing we need. What does this look like? Most people need healing and freedom from: *The Glory Days, Regrets Over Missed Opportunities,* and *Healing from Past Pain.*

The Glory Days refer to the belief that one's best days are behind them. It could be from your childhood, high school, college, a past job, a past relationship, a past achievement, a place you lived, a position you had, or a mountaintop you experienced. The problem is a person has the belief that the best days were the former days. This becomes a stumbling block to the future when a person tries to relive them, recreate them, or have remorse that they didn't know enough to enjoy it while it was happening. A person ends up feeling like the best part of their story has already been told. With that belief, it isn't hard to see how someone can become angry, frustrated, restless, or just plain defeated.

Regrets Over Missed Opportunities speaks about how life "would have been" if different decisions or outcomes taken place. When a person looks back at fork in the road, there can be a deep belief that the wrong choice was selected. Instead of reliving the past, people are kicking themselves over the life they believe they should have had. Did they choose the right career, the right spouse, the right place to go to school, the right pursuits, the right financial decisions, and so on? People in this place can conclude they are living the consolation prize life instead of the gold medal one they could have had. The self-loathing, recriminations, and regrets from this can cast a grey cloud over someone's life. A person can feel trapped and have no one to blame but the one staring at them in the mirror every morning.

The need for *Healing Over Past Pain* happens when a person is dragging the hurts of the past along with them into their present tense. The pain is real, intense, and can seem overwhelming. Some have been victims of abuse, neglect, betrayal, rejection, or deception. Other people battered their lives at some point in the past, and it is hard to see a path forward. Without deep healing, some choose to survive, protect oneself by keeping others at a distance, or punish the ones around you today for what someone else did yesterday.

Healing over past pain doesn't stop with what others have done. Some aren't just carrying the pain caused by others, but they also carrying the regrets over the pain they caused. Like a coin, the side called "victim" has been flipped to "victimizer." They inflicted hurt and did to someone else what they promised they never would do to a person. Granted, some who inflicted pain didn't have this self-awareness. Blinded by selfishness or choosing to be dismissive of others, people were steamrolled, swept aside, or just used for their personal gain or temporary pleasure. Only down the road do some look back and realize the carnage left in their wake.

Whether it's the pain of others' actions or the regret over the pain caused by one's own actions, it can become a heavy weight that holds people back, keeps them down, or exhausts them with the weight of carrying this burden through life. These three expressions are all part of *Redeeming Your Past*.

After reading these options, one may ask, "What if I see the need in more than one or in all of the areas?" You aren't abnormal and you aren't alone. If most were being brutally honest with themselves, God, and others, they would say the same thing. I know Barb and I did as we faced the need for our own healing. The purpose of this book though, isn't just to agree we have the same types of wounds. Although not feeling alone helps, please don't settle for that. The goal is to experience and discover the path to healing.

Your past glory days don't have to be your best days. Your regret over past opportunities doesn't have to be the lingering disappointment hanging over today. You do not have to have a consolation-prize life. The pain caused by others, yourself, or both doesn't have to be the identity you carry moving forward. You can experience healing, forgiveness, and freedom. There is a big difference walking through life with scars versus open infected wounds. A scar is external evidence that internal healing has taken place. It tells a story of healing and rebirth. Infected wounds tell a story of defeat or the past pulling the strings and controlling life.

In the coming chapters, we want to walk with you and share some lessons we have learned along the way and how we experienced God *Redeeming Our Past*. Many stories are from Kevin's life. Not because he is more interesting than Barb, but because they are ones we chose to help tell this story. The goal is for you to find connection points in your story. By peeling back some of our layers, our hope is that you will feel safe to do the same. Remember, we want more for you, and so does God.

***

As we move from here, let's lay out a few guiding points now that will help us throughout this journey. First, we will address these three areas of healing at different points throughout the book. They are like threads woven through the chapters, just like our lives are the woven threads of our experiences and relationships. Because of this, you may connect with this book at different points because of the unique aspects of your own story. We hope you will think about yours as you read portions of ours. There will be principles that all can use, but the application will connect uniquely to each person's place in life.

Second, not all of the stories that will be shared were paved on easy street. I wish I could say that all my life lessons were learned through successes and I could say, "Do what I do, and you will get what I get." Frankly, many lessons were learned through failure, heartbreak, and deep soul searching. I do admire those who are successes. But I also relate to those who know what it is to fall down and get back up. We need both in our lives. Successful people teach us what to emulate. Those who have failed and gotten back up often teach what to avoid or how to respond to difficulty. Most people's stories are a combination of both. That is why the first part of Proverbs 24:16 encourages me. It says, "For a righteous *man* may fall seven times and rises again." Much of life is what happens after we fall and decide to rise up again.

Third, the goal is to point you to God and His power to *Redeem Your Past* and show the path of healing from the *Glory Days, Past Regrets,* and *Past Pain*. We are not trying to paint ourselves as the heroes of the story. Jesus Christ is the hero who came and rescued the human race. There is an important reason I share this at the outset. An author warned me that many get turned off reading books that share personal weakness and stories of falling down. His words communicated to me that some people want to look up to someone, not be disappointed in what they have done. Our story is one of healing, hope, and redemption, but I admit up front, you have to be okay with seeing some of the struggles. After the struggles, God's forgiveness, redemption, and healing are on full display. Our hope is that you will conclude how amazing God is, and that no matter where you are in life, there can be a *Redeeming of Your Past*. I am going to optimistically conclude that you will be ok with a story that includes both successes and getting back up after failure.

So, with that said, let's move forward together. Our deepest desire and prayer for you is for you to experience the healing of the *Redeeming of Your Past*.

Chapter One

Laying Some Groundwork

T hink of the last time you had the window seat on an airplane at cruising altitude. The world looks very different looking out the window at 30,000-35,000 feet. It is fascinating to see the organized patterns as you fly over Midwestern farmland or the rugged terrain as you go over the Rocky Mountains. You can't see the houses and highways, but you have a clearer view of the "big picture." That was the objective in the introduction. We ascend to a higher view for an overview of the journey we are embarking on together.

Introducing the *Glory Days, Regrets Over Missed Opportunities,* and *Healing from Past Pain* are part of that. Now, it is essential to descend our plane to a lower cruising altitude for a moment so we can make out a bit more of the detail. Understanding what these three areas of needed redemption can look like in daily life is helpful. The purpose is to provide tools for you to be reflecting over your life as we work through God's design in *Redeeming Your Past*. I will give examples of these in my life's story. As I do, see if your mind recalls moments and memories from your life. This will give you a frame of reference as we move forward. Our flight plan is a destination of greater healing, freedom, and effectiveness in your life.

Glory Days

Sometimes, we know when we are in a sweet spot in life. Everything is humming along, and we take it all in with intentionality and appreciation. It is kind of like stopping to take in a great sunset that strikes you in a moment. Your mind, emotions, and spirit all engage together to write a memory in the long-term file of your brain. Other times, we don't recognize the good times until we look back some time later. Only then do we realize we should have taken more time to smell the roses. We can recognize the glory days both

1

in the moment, and in the rearview mirror of life.

For me, childhood and adolescent athletics and academics were like that. It all came easy to me. I excelled at both and didn't appreciate the gift of it. I just thought I would always win more than I lost. I expected to succeed most of the time, and it was a time where I gained new skills and absorbed new subjects quickly. When I learned to play baseball, it was a childhood love. After my dad, brother, and I worked at it for a year or so, it became like the childhood game of *Sandlot*. Years later I went out for the high school team in 10th grade, not having played on an organized team for five years. At my first at bat, I hit a double and went on to bat .400 that season. I thought it would always be that way.

In school, A's weren't hard to come by. With little effort, I made honor rolls, and had a 3.9 GPA in high school. I think I assumed intellectual pursuits were easy. Probably a combination of naivety and a bit of arrogance. Then college came along. I attended a liberal arts school that was one of top 50 in the country. During the first semester, I handed in a paper and received a D. The professor wrote in red, "The next time you write it the night before, please don't make it so obvious." Ouch. In sports, I was on a partial scholarship and thought I would excel right away. I was fifth out of five goalies on the depth chart. During my first training camp, a varsity starter almost broke my jaw with the force of his shot. He had spent some time on the junior national team of Cameroon, and it showed.

The glory days of high school disappeared into the horizon and I was left with the reality that everyone at the school was very smart, and the athletes were all talented. It became clear that I had taken for granted the opportunities I had in high school. Imagine where I would have been had I added a strong work ethic to academic abilities. What would have been the result had I prepared the summer before my first training camp like I should have? There was definitely some sadness over those lost glory days. I had two choices - either get bitter or get better. In sports, I gave my best. It didn't quite work out the way I hoped, but at least I knew I had tried my best by the time my college career was over. In academics, I resisted working my hardest, and skated through as an average student who should have been better.

You get the idea. I looked back at my high school years and wished I could have re-created the ease of success and enjoyed it more fully while I had it. As a young adult, I didn't quite learn the full lesson, and the cycle repeated itself in early adult life. I wouldn't recognize great times until reflecting back later and then would bemoan what I didn't have. The *Glory Days*, if not properly processed, can lead to a lack of contentment.

When Barb and I didn't have much in the early years, we had to be creative and enjoy life without having money. Later, I realized there was a simple joy to those years, and I should have appreciated them. In my twenties, I received lots of affirmation for being a good, young pastor. Funny how that changed as I got older. Expectations changed, and I didn't quite live up to them for large chunks of time. By the time I reached my forties, I was burned out and bitter that I hadn't succeeded like when I was younger in ministry. No one was more disappointed in me than me. Whatever the source, the *Glory Days* are marked by looking back and wishing you could recreate what used to be at the expense of appreciating what is in the here and now. When you don't get past this, it leads to beating yourself for not recognizing how good you had it, often at the expense of not recognizing the good of today. The *Glory Days* result in us often missing the gift of this day.

Regrets Over Missed Opportunities

When you look back and realize you may have chosen the wrong fork in the road, there can be inner sadness, frustration, and anger over the choice you made. People can reflect on jobs, relationships, schools, places they lived, friends they chose, deeds they did, or regret their choice of resisting a relationship with God.

For me, my regrets centered on decisions I made when I lacked inner confidence and needed the approval of others to validate me. I look back and realize I had been second best in many areas because I deferred to others with more confidence, and as a result, so did others. In ministry, I realized I should have had a second job much of the time because the churches I served didn't pay that well. Instead, I thought I was being a good, sacrificial pastor in putting all my energy in trying to help struggling churches turn around. My family suffered financially, and I regretted not being a better provider later in life.

There were times I believe I missed opportunities for God's best because I wanted to keep Barb and the kids happy by not moving and demonstrate that I was a loyal pastor to the church by staying longer than the average pastor stayed. I looked back and believed I missed the whispers of God to serve in missions for a time. By not taking new opportunities to serve, I missed chances to grow in leadership and capacity. I let finances stand in the way of getting further education. You see the trend. The regret over perceived missed opportunities can cause one to be condemning of self, and bitter toward present circumstances.

It took me a long time to realize a couple of things. First, just because I thought I missed opportunities doesn't mean I did in every case. No one can live life on target while looking back. Jesus had something to say about that when he compared it to trying to plow a field while looking back. You can't plow straight because you aren't looking where you are supposed to be looking. Second, even if I did miss some opportunities, it doesn't mean that God isn't big enough to pour out His grace and still accomplish His will in my life and for others. I realized that even if I did stay at one church too long, God still worked it out that my two older kids met their spouses because I stayed eighteen years at one church. That is something worth being grateful to God for. I do believe I missed opportunities and could have been a better pastor, provider, and leader at points throughout that time. God was bigger than all of that and still blessed my kids with wonderful spouses. Unfortunately, the regret over missing opportunities led to me not seeing soon enough that God's grace and power still made sure my kids were in the right place at the right time. I was in my pit of despair way too long.

Are there missed opportunities, both real and perceived, that nag at you?

Healing Over Past Pain

As I stood before 200+ people on that Sunday morning, the humiliation and horror was staring me in the eyes. I looked down to my right, and there sat my wife, steeling herself for this terrible moment. Next to her were my two daughters. They bravely sat by their mother, giving love and support to her. I thought for a moment how grateful I was that my youngest son was back East on an early summer trip, visiting with my parents and my oldest son and our daughter-in-law.

It was Father's Day, and this moment was happening. I

4

looked out and saw board members dotting the crowd. They had pained looks on their faces, as they braced themselves for something that had to happen, but none of us wanted. They had been thrust into a horrible leadership burden, and they had no choice in the matter. As I scanned the crowd, I saw those who knew something was up but had no idea of what I was about to do. Others sat there knowingly, either from their conversations with me the week prior or having heard the rumors and speculation leading up to Sunday's service.

I looked left to right across the semicircle layout of the sanctuary with my eyes landing on my district superintendent and his wife. He had trusted me with so much, and I had betrayed that trust. Yet, there he was, balancing his responsibility to the local church with his genuine heart to help and show grace to Barb, the kids, and myself. He was about to be handed the reins to a hurting church, and he didn't deserve this.

Although I was fully clothed, it felt like I was completely naked. After twenty-five years and 2,500 sermons, I was about to preach the one I never thought I would have to and there was no one to blame but myself. In an effort to protect Barb and the kids, as well as the church, the message had been prewritten and prescreened by my wife and our district superintendent. It was a completely truthful confession about the burnout in my life and my need to step away from ministry. It would allude to behaviors and problems in my life that necessitated this moment, but it would share a boundary that the details about my action were known by my family, the board, my superintendent, and select others. Although it was a moment meant to protect others as much as possible, I knew that more would know the "rest of the story" in the days ahead. How did I get here, and why did so many have to suffer because of what I had done?

Although maybe not as public and dramatic, I imagine many of you who are starting this journey can relate to moments of shame and bewilderment. Far too often, we come to places where we wonder how we got there. It could be shattering betrayal, a humiliating termination at work, the untold suffering of abuse, the enslaving grip of addiction, or the defeat of having given your best only to experience crushing defeat. Whether the delusion of self-reliance has deceived you or the shame of self-destruction has brought you low, many, if not most, know what it is to have the mask of your carefully constructed reality come crashing down. I believe every person will need healing from past pain at some point in their lives, if not multiple times.

Although the example I shared focused on pain I caused, it can be just as true for pain caused by others. It is my belief that most people's wounds come from pain that is both self-inflicted and inflicted by others. Whether you ask, "Why did they do that?" or "How could I have done that?" past pain is something we often wish we could fly over, but we have to deal with it at some point.

How about you? Is there past pain you caused, or had inflicted on you, that is still an open wound, instead of a scar that has been healed?

Bringing It Together

Redeeming the Past can be for a variety of reasons. Regardless of your reason for picking up this book, thanks for being here. Whether curious or crushed, you are a welcome participant in this journey. In the pages ahead, you will hear more about how God wants to and can *Redeem Your Past*. This journey was something I feared and yearned for at the same time. Maybe you do as well. We can often cover up with our masks, but on some level we know something is wrong. By mask, I am referring to the portrait or impression each person wants others to see and believe when they relate to us. Masks can be made up of truth and lies. They can tell parts of our story that reveal what we want, but rarely do they tell the whole story. Masks are used to hide hurts, fears, truth, and lies we don't want others to know. We can even use masks to hide from ourselves.

***

In the end, though, we come to moments in our lives where we see that our masks fail us. Whether these moments come from revelation, exhaustion, or failure, they will come. The key is what each one of us chooses to do in these moments. Each moment when our masks fall off provides an opportunity to grow or regress. If we buy the lie that masks protect us and those we love, then we will hastily pick it back up and reattach it. If we see unmasking as a way of becoming free to become who God truly created us to be, then it can be transforming. You don't have to remain gripped, misdirected, or held back by Glory Days, Regrets Over Missed Opportunities, and Past Pain that has left perpetual wounds.

The chapters that follow are meant to be an encouragement, but this isn't a call to self-help. Self-reliance won't get you where you need to go. The stories I share are also not an expression of self-loathing because self-hatred won't bring healing. This book is an invitation to a God-led journey in which you can experience freedom, insight, and the joy of becoming more of who you were created to be. We all are on a journey. Thank you for spending some time travelling down this healing road together. I believe you will find it time well spent.

Chapter Two

We All Have a Story

Throughout each one's life story, there are places where we see two types of influences. One is the movement of God where He reveals Himself to us, give us grace, reveals His plan, and provides unexplained moments of Divine intervention. I call this the fingerprints of God. The second are moments marked by deceptive messages delivered during our broken or vulnerable moments. These moments of deception leave an impression, either due to the deep pain or temporary pleasure associated with the event. I call these the whispers of the deceiver.

Both types of influences can mark us for a lifetime. One can build faith and a sense of purpose. The other will break faith and our connection to God and His divine purpose. Discerning between the two is vital. The problem arises when we make decisions or choose directions based on faulty conclusions. For instance, some experience a difficult circumstance and conclude something about God that isn't true. The enemy whispered a deception. On the other hand, there are those who received blessings from God and chalk it up to the results of their work or luck. Rather than thank God, they thank themselves or their "lucky stars." Learning to sift is essential, because we often chart our lives on how we "read" the conclusions we make from key life events.

Jeremiah, the prophet, was told by the Lord to sift "the precious from the vile." What a fantastic word picture - the precious and the vile. I believe *Redeeming the Past* is significantly impacted by how effectively or ineffectively we sift these two opposites. So, what does separating the precious from the vile look like? It involves reflecting and remembering key moments and events from our lives and evaluating the conclusions we drew from them. Were they whispers from God or the lies from the deceiver? Did we conclude the right things about God and the right things about others? It is an interaction of one's mind, emotions, will, and spirit. With the compass of God's Word and His Spirit, plus a willingness to be honest with ourselves, we can decipher these key moments.

With that being said, let me give a caution and a comfort. First, the caution. If a memory is so painful and impacting that you can't keep your emotions from leading the way on this journey, it may be necessary to have a skilled counselor help in your process. For me, having a trained counselor who shared my worldview as a Christian helped me be more at ease. When Barb and I went through marriage counseling after my moral failure, there were some pains that were very deep for us both. We had a hard time talking to each other about it, let alone thinking about it clearly. Our counselor walked us, individually (without the other person present) through Eye Movement Desensitization and Reprocessing therapy (EMDR), a process developed in the treatment of war veterans who went through significant loss and trauma. It is a process that helps remap the brain as it processes through deep pain and loss. It enables the brain to process it with both the left and right sides. As our counselor put it, it allows one to not just feel the event with its associated pain, but also think through it as well. It balances the perspective so that it can be processed in a way that leads towards progress and healing. I am not saying this is necessary for everyone, but I am saying we had moments that we couldn't process with a clear mind or from God's perspective. I don't want to send you on a journey by yourself that might be best taken with a trusted, skilled helper. Consider this as you read this chapter.

The comfort is to remember the Holy Spirit promises to be a comforter, healer, guide, and teacher in our healing journeys as well. In addition to a skilled human counselor, the Holy Spirit led Barb and I to a church with a great pastor. He and his wife spoke into our lives as they were prompted by the Holy Spirit. They spoke prophetic words, encouraging words, words of wisdom, and prayed powerfully and right on point. The Holy Spirit worked through them. He also worked through men and women in the church who lifted us up, spoke words of life, and pointed us to the Lord. The Holy Spirit also spoke to us through our prayer times, both privately, and with each other. He spoke through the Scriptures. He spoke through worship music. He spoke through marriage ministries like Marriage Today, and Love and Respect. The Holy Spirit spoke, comforted, healed, helped, and transformed us and our view of the past. I would encourage you to embrace the role of the Holy Spirit in helping you heal from the past. God used His Spirit, a godly and skilled counselor, a life-giving church, and the ministries and music of others we never met. The caution and the comfort have a similar point: don't feel you have to go it alone, and be careful to recognize when you need another godly, informed perspective to help you sift what is mixed together.

In the remaining pages of this chapter, I will review some of the key moments in my life to this point in which I had to do some sifting. Some will be fingerprints of God, and others will be the whispers of the deceiver. The hope is that you will see the need in your life to do the same sifting and reflection in order to know if the decisions you have made and the direction you have taken are based on the right information and whose voice has tended to have sway in your life.

I admit there was a hesitancy to writing this chapter. Everyone has a story, and I sure don't want to come across as if mine is more valuable than someone else's. No one wants to be a blinded narcissist who thinks the world is all about "me." It's like the person who takes to many "selfies," clearly communicating they are the center of wherever they are. My prayer is by sharing selected stories from my life, the Holy Spirit will bring memories to your mind. If you struggle with your relationship and view of God, remember He loves you and wants to help you. He takes you right where you are. He just loves you too much to leave you there.

If we don't sift the fingerprints from the whispers, we become a muddled mess of contradiction. We are driven by the blessings and purposes of God's fingerprints; yet the blind spots caused by listening to the deceiver's whispers lead to crashes or detours on life's journey. If we can learn to tune out the whispers of deception, while intently focusing on God's fingerprints, we will see with greater clarity the events that have brought us to this point and the road God has marked out before us. Thanks for reading through this important groundwork. Now, some of the rest of the story.

At ages seven-to-eight, both the fingerprints and the whispers were there. Although too young to understand it all in its fullest sense, there was a sense of good and evil in the world around me. When a teenage boy began to show me his dad's pornographic magazines, it was curious to me; yet there was something sick about it. The day he tried to molest me revealed the evil behind the whispers. At the same time, God broke it with a fingerprint. Someone came home, and I was able to escape, never to return to his house again. He rescued me that day when the boy's mom got home. It was turning bad very quickly, and I could feel a wave of helplessness encompass me. I didn't know who God was at this point, but His fingerprints were there.

During this same time of life, I chose vulgar cursing, stealing, and attempts at acceptance in the neighborhood. The enemy's whispers were there. I heard messages of rejection, as well as the lure of pornography and in some of the behavior of the people around me. At the same time, I also saw the fingerprints of God. His Holy Spirit began to draw me. I remember the day He spoke into my mind and heart that I didn't need to curse and swear. Although I didn't recognize Him, He knew me and was starting to speak to me before I understood it was His Spirit speaking to me.

As you can see, my life was marked by both during this season. Because of shame and secrecy, I never told anyone about the pornography and partial assault until later in my teen years. Tragically, the early exposure to pornography and sex impacted my life for years to come. Instead of seeking help to process the images that were put onto my hard drive, I would periodically seek to look at more throughout my teen years. Although I avoided pornography from my wedding until a crash at forty-four, my mind had a struggle with lust that I struggled with throughout my adult life. As to the fingerprints, God used the early memories of His protection to draw me and to press onto my life the understanding that He walks with me, talks with me, and sees everything. With grace, He has forgiven me, and strengthens me daily.

At fourteen and fifteen, God spoke clearly into my life and introduced me to truths that would mark me for the rest of my life. In December of 1984, He placed a calling on my life for pastoral ministry. At a youth retreat near Divide, Colorado, He spoke so clearly that I thought someone behind me was talking to me. When I turned, no one was there, and I realized that He was communicating with me that I was to be a pastor.

A few months later, a beautiful teenage girl came to the wonderful, yet somewhat surprising conclusion that she was attracted to me. She remembers the day she saw me at church and noticed me, even though I had walked past her and been in the same youth group for over a year. Even though I moved less than a year later and I was 2,000 miles away, she kept a memory of me. That can only be credited to the Lord. I wasn't someone to notice, was unaware of how to speak to her heart, and was full of insecurities and baggage; yet, she saw something in me. Three years later, God used my wallet being stolen in New Jersey to reconnect us. After it was stolen, it was later found by someone, and mailed to her school in Colorado. This event reintroduced us to each other. His fingerprints were all over our courtship and marriage. Barbara Duckworth becoming Barbara Goos was clearly a gift from God.

Yet, in spite of all these fingerprints, distorted lies were still in the background. As a teenager at a sleepover with some guys, we spent a good part of the late-night hours watching pornographic movies while the friend's parents slept. I knew it was wrong, but I had continued to keep the pain of the past and the struggles of the present a secret. This led to more sin in the months to come. Crushed, filled with self-hatred and a sense of inadequacy, I was conflicted. On one hand, the fingerprints of God had marked my life with a calling to serve Him in ministry for the rest of my life. He had introduced me to my first love, who, unbeknownst to me, would one day be my wife. On the other hand, the sins committed against me and the sins I had committed were a fog of distortion and contradiction. Due to a fear of rejection and my firm belief of condemnation, I kept it all to myself and told no one. This prevented the necessary sifting of the precious from the vile in my life and the lives of others.

I hope you see in these examples that God's fingerprints are marking lives, while at the same time, the enemy of our soul is trying to lie, wound, and distort our vision. He seeks to cloud our vision of God's fingerprints by evil lies and deceptions. The pattern of struggling with my distorted thinking in the secret places of my life while openly striving to serve God and my family was an ongoing cycle. The highs of God's love and blessings were amazing. The depths of my lows weighed me down. The secret struggle in my mind distorted my view of God's gift of a wonderful wife. It resulted in me choosing to be critical of her on far too many occasions and becoming really good at condemning myself, even to the point of self-hatred at moments.

Throughout the first twenty years of marriage and ministry, I spent years performing and pining for success and breakthrough, believing the distorted lies that I had to make things happen and perform well for others to befriend me, love me, or stay in the churches I served. It led to the conflict of having a heart committed to the Lord, and my family, while also struggling with insecurities and fears. Let me illustrate.

God gave me a heart to be a committed father, and I thoroughly enjoy being a father to my four kids— God's fingerprints. Unfortunately, I felt that my kids didn't appreciate the home they had and thought I was looked down upon by them - distorted lies. My heart yearned for people to know Jesus Christ as their Lord and grow in Him to maturity and the fullness of His plan for them—God's fingerprints. I was too gripped by needing the approval of others and was a peacekeeper at times instead of a peacemaker—distorted lies.

I wanted to see the best in people and believe they could change and be transformed in Christ—God's fingerprints. At times, I avoided confronting people about their lives when they were blinded to their weaknesses, in order to maintain friendship with them or have approval from them—distorted lies. I was given talents by God in academics and thinking on things deeply- -God's fingerprints. In school, I would do enough to get by and be satisfied by the compliments of good grades even though I didn't give my best— distorted lies. You get the point. Far too often, our story is littered with lies that dilute or distract from the reality of the fingerprints of God.

What should have happened years earlier was an openness with the right people and with God that I had distorted thinking and sin struggles. Although I had accountability partners and mentors throughout my adult life, I would let them in pretty far, but not into the inner core. Thus, victories and progress would only go so far, but still leave deep roots in place. I would pull big chunks of the dandelions and not get all their roots. Then it would resurface weeks, months, or years later. When I did finally break and go through the process of it being pulled out from the root, it was after my private struggles became public. It was involuntary, and as a result, I broke the trust of many. In spite of the horrible pain I caused, God poured out His grace and mercy. Almost everyone I confessed to chose to give grace, even though they were hurt, disappointed, or surprised. That isn't to say every relationship survived long-term. Most didn't make it, but the journey of deep healing taught me that when the precious and vile are sifted, life can be lived as never before.

It was a lesson learned the hard way, but God revealed something important when I had to start over after my resignation. The world didn't collapse. My worst fears weren't realized. Yes, the secrecy of my sin did result in having to rebuild trust. It would have been much better if I had let the right people in at an earlier point in my life. It would have been better to let trustworthy helpers see into the core of my struggles with all its distorted thinking, personal pain, and sin.

Yet, it turns out my worst fears were unfounded. There were a core of people who saw it all, forgave, and pushed me to move forward. Unfortunately, the delay in doing this meant more sins and wounds committed against others, and there was an accountability for that, as was right. But God brought a new beginning as He taught me to sift the precious from the vile, the fingerprints of God from the whispers of the deceiver. This idea of making sure we recognize the difference between the fingerprints and the distorted lies is critical. Far too often, God gets blame He doesn't deserve but doesn't get credit He does deserve. Meanwhile, the distorted whispers cloud our minds and skew our perspectives. It can manifest itself in various ways.

A person walks away from his childhood with a negative experience about having to go to church. Rather than see the fingerprints of God marking his life with a foundation of truth, the person focuses on the imperfections of his family from Monday-Saturday. He or she listens to the whispers of the deceiver that faith in God is really nothing more than man-made religion meant to oppress and enslave. He chooses a path called freethinking or enlightenment in which he thinks he is being delivered from superstition. He outgrows God, so to speak.

So, instead of seeing the fingerprint and sifting out the human imperfections around him, the man attributes these imperfections to God Himself. He may not continue to believe in Him at all. The pursuit of life, family, career, and financial goals takes over his focus. The next thing you know, decades have passed, and his kids are raised. Sadly though, in the desire to raise his kids to be

14

free of any religious teaching or God talk, they now lack the foundation he had. He walked away from his foundation, but his kids' foundation of faith in God was excluded from their formative years.

Later, as an empty nester, he now begins to think about the ultimate meaning of his life as he sees the finish line of life a whole lot closer than ever before. The angry musings of youth don't have the same passion in midlife, and with the hostility waning, he begins to notice the fingerprints of God again. God stirs his heart and woos him back. God had never left the scene. Years down the road, the man does the sifting and sorting that should have happened decades earlier. He still wants no part of some stifled religion based on people's traditions and preferences. Good call. Instead, he experiences a living, personal relationship with Jesus Christ that is integrated into his entire life. It becomes a healing salve to the wounds of life, and he can now connect with other Christians in a life-giving church. He is back home with his Father where he was always welcome and wanted.

Although his story will have a great ending, the man realizes that he failed his kids terribly. Instead of faith, he gave his kids a skeptical attitude toward God at best, or a disbelief in Him at worst. The fingerprints of God are all around them, but they don't see it. Dad tries to communicate with them, but his voice struggles to penetrate the walls he helped build. Are his kids a lost cause? Of course not. God loves those kids and can break down those walls. The man though, has the regrets that he let his decision to listen to deceptive whispers help form his parenting priorities, rather than the fingerprints and Truth of God.

God loves this man's kids and will woo them the way He wooed the man. The names and faces changed over the years, but I have seen this scenario play out with too great a frequency. This isn't the end of the story, but it does illustrate the regrettable and tragic consequences of not sorting out the distorted lies of the enemy from the fingerprints of God. Frankly, many people will grieve how they negatively impacted their children out of their own broken places. It doesn't have to be the end of the story, but it does illustrate the need to sift the precious from the vile as soon as possible.

So, now what? Well, that depends. If you are the parent of adult children who were failed by your listening to the distorted whispers, humility is better than badgering your kids. Assuaging your guilt by being too intense with them won't be as effective as a humble confession. Be willing to share your life journey, and how you saw things through a distorted lens. Confess your selfishness, stubbornness, and pride. Admit to your kids that you gave them many things but not what mattered most. Explain that although you won't badger them into a relationship with Christ, you are praying that your life example from here on out will show the difference He makes.

After admitting your imperfections, put your heart's desire on the Lord and ask Him to help you live as one who has been forgiven. It makes the focus on loving Him and living out His gift. Pray for your kids and grandkids. Be an active part of their lives. Love them right where they are and trust that the same God that never gave up on you will never give up on them. Be careful to avoid actions that come from a sense of desperation or impatience. The Holy Spirit will give you opportunities to speak to them and live for Him in front of them.

Hopefully, my personal stories and the "not so hypothetical example" demonstrates the necessity of sifting the distorting lies so you can see the fingerprints of God. Take that extended example of that man's journey and apply the principles to any place in life where the sifting is needed. Wherever you are and whatever your station in life, a commitment to lifelong, Spirit-led learning is key. I had a mentoring pastor in my life who would pray this prayer, "Lord, help me see my blind spots before others do." If we don't see them first, others do and are impacted by the decisions we have made because of them.

***

Our decisions now can either break the bonds of the past or perpetuate past failures into ongoing behavior. The person whose generations are littered with brokenness can be the one who says, "No more!" and starts a new path for the generations that follow. Enslavement can give way to freedom. Victims can become victorious. The oppressed can become overcomers. The proud can become humble. Grace can be all-sufficient.

Or . . . you can blindly perpetuate your problems to others. The person who has been hurt can become emotionally detached and end up punishing the ones who didn't commit the sin. People can become controlling as a way of compensating for their past and

16

impair the next generation's ability to make decisions and do life as God intended. Addiction can continue, abuse can perpetuate, and blind spots can lead to a relational demolition derby. Or . . . God can help you sift the precious from the vile and open up a whole new world that He has for you.

Really, the choice is up to you, just as it was up to me. There is the precious to be cherished and the vile to be extracted. The fingerprints of God are all around you, as are the deceptive lies of the enemy. When you hear both speaking, which will you listen to moving forward from here?

Chapter Three
Life Testimony

I f someone was tallying the number of times I have hit the backspace key to correct something while I was typing on a computer, it would be a large number. If you offered me a dollar for every hit of the backspace key, my mistakes in the past would be an investment for the future. That's exactly what they can be, but life isn't that clean cut or simple. God never wants us to excuse past sin just because He is good at turning things to good when we submit to Him (See Romans 6:1-2). Second, some mistakes are so painful or embarrassing, the correction process is painstaking.

It reminds me of when I was learning to type in high school. Typing? Yes, before texting was keyboarding on a computer, which used to sit on desk. Before that, there was an electric machine called a typewriter. The IBM "Selectric" made an unmistakable clacking sound when you typed. Still don't understand? Well, go get me my cassette tapes, so I can listen to America's Top Forty with Casey Kasem while wearing a pink polo shirt. Okay, back to the typewriter.

Our high school teacher wanted us to understand the painful experience of correcting mistakes, so she had the school get very old typewriters that were manual (not electric) for us to learn. Whenever we make a mistake, we had to take a small rectangle, white correction strip (anyone remember "White-Out"?) and put it over the letter we mistyped. When you retyped the letter, it would press the white-out strip and cover your mistake. Sound painfully slow? It was.

Just like that old typewriter in Mrs. Petrov's classroom, hitting the backspace in life is hard. We can't really go back and change what we have done. What we try to do is make amends, rebuild trust, learn lessons, get back up and try harder to do it right the next time. In the midst of this pursuit, one may wonder where our relationship with God is in all this. God is right in the middle of it, helping us learn that although He never approves of willful wrongdoing, He is never caught by surprise. He is able to redeem the past, without approving of the wrong that was done. It is an amazing mystery of His power that He knows all, yet no one can blame Him for the choices he or she has made. He knows, leads, corrects, forgives, restores, and redeems. That includes regrets over missed opportunities and healing past pain caused by others and self. It isn't condoning wrongdoing. It is celebrating that there is One who is greater than every sin, which is a great hope when life's backspace button doesn't work. Looking back can give us a good view of our pitfalls. Looking up to Him can give us a good view of His power. If we could learn to see our lives through the lens of eternity, it would give us hope. Not a hope that results in a casual view of hurting ourselves or others. No. Any truly repentant person would do about anything to go back and undo the damage they caused. Looking at God's eternal power though, can remind us that failure doesn't have to be final. Let's dig into some of this hope.

"All my days were written in your book, before there was one of them." As the ancient Jewish King David reflected on the unfolding of God's plan in His life, he made this Scriptural declaration and promise. Inspired by the Spirit of God, it became more than a truth for David's time and his life. This promise is true for every person, in every place, at every time. Every person was created on purpose by God and is part of His divine purpose for the world.

What differs for each person is how His declarations weave their way into each one's life personally. It is a heady idea to consider that your life is so uniquely designed that God has put His design for you down in writing. Instead of living as if life is nothing more than a random gasp for survival, each person can come to grips with the notion of a personal identity to be discovered as a son or daughter of the Father. Robert Henderson writes about discovering and acting upon God's specific plans for each person in his book *Operating in the Courts of Heaven*. Another great author on this is Jack Frost (not the winter guy), in his two books on our unique identity with our Father in heaven.

I believe the Scriptures to be true and that each of us has a book, a destiny, for our lives. It is all that God has declared and planned for each of us. A central purpose of life then is to seek, understand, and pursue a relationship with the One who has declared things for us and learn to obey what He has written. When Jesus' disciples asked Him to teach them how to pray, He addresses the central need of people to align themselves with God's purposes in daily life. Jesus prayed, "Your Kingdom come, Your will be done, on earth, as it is in heaven."

Pursuing the "how" and "what" of that prayer is its own discussion. There are many opinions and teachings on this. Although important in its own right, that conversation isn't the target in this chapter. For the sake of our journey, let's agree on the foundational truth that God has a specific plan for each person, even if we may have differing thoughts on the process of discovering, understanding, and living it out.

With that in place, we can admit that most of us have found it a challenge, at times, to understand His plan. For some, it has been difficult to willingly submit to His plans when we have wanted something different. Sometimes people have other desires or prefer shortcuts to achieving the goal. When we do this, we can mess up our lives and impact others as well. The turning of the pages of our destiny can slow to a stall, and the pages of life get stuck. Stuck in a repeating chapter of something from the past — a glory day we can't repeat or a regret we can't undo. Living life in a stalled place is no fun. There is good news though. None of us has to remain in that place. Each of our lives can be a story of God working and moving to lead us to a page-turning miracle of His power, love, and grace. If we get stuck, He can get us unstuck, even if we aren't sure how that happens at times.

We get unstuck when we patiently pursue Him to guide us when we don't know what to do, and wholeheartedly obey Him when we do know what to do. The pages of our book move according to His plan when we are in this place of submission to Him. Recognizing what this looks like in the daily grind of life is essential. The Holy Spirit's leading in our lives can be subtle one moment, yet crystal clear at others. As we learn to recognize His voice, see the evidence of His fingerprints, and follow His moving, the volume of our lives can become quite a page-turner. If we learn to trust that He is the right One to be in charge, we can see His leading in the here and now, and redeeming the past as well.

Let me share a few moments from my life that illustrate a few page-turning moments. In upcoming chapters, I will also share when I got stuck of my own doing. As I recount both, the hope is you will allow your mind to wander over the pages of the book of your own life. It is good to see where God has been moving the pages and to recognize when we have gotten in our own way. Both teach lessons that are vital to learn. As I share moments from my story, reflect on yours as well and remember, our focus is about Redeeming the Past.

Protection

A key moment for me happened when I was five years old. I was riding in the passenger seat of a car while cruising down a highway. While I don't remember how it happened (leaning on the door or messing with the handle), my passenger door suddenly swung open. The feeling of that moment is something I haven't forgotten to this day. I didn't scream but was frozen in disbelief as I watched the painted line on the pavement whizz by, while hearing the low hum of the tires on the asphalt. These were the days prior to car seats beyond infancy and the emphasis on seatbelts at all times. The suction of the air being drawn out the open door began to pull me toward the open door. My foot dangled close to the road and I remember thinking I was about to fall out of the car. There was a strange calm juxtaposed with shock and fear. Suddenly, the arm of my mother's boyfriend pulled me toward him and shut the door with force. I didn't really know God at this young age, but I can look back and see He saved me.

It didn't stop there though. At seven or eight years of age, I was on weekend visitation with my dad. My parents had separated before I was two years old and were divorced by this point. Through a series of events, my older brother lived with my father, and I was with my mother. We had moved back to New Jersey after two years of being in the Western United States, which allowed me to reconnect with family. Every other weekend was spent with my dad, stepmom, and brother. During one of these visits, God's protection was evident once again.

My older brother and I were playing with the neighborhood

kids at a pond that had frozen over during a cold snap. While we all goofed off on the ice, some of the kids thought it would be entertaining to start breaking apart the ice at the shoreline. The pond dropped off and didn't have any beach to speak of. The game was to jump over the exposed area onto dry ground. Not exactly our best choice of games. When my turn came, I had this uneasy feeling but didn't want to be shown up in front of the guys, even though we "guys" were just boys. Giving into peer pressure was a second bad decision that day.

As I got ready to jump, my feet slipped out from under me, and I ended up with my butt in the water and my arms and legs straddling the ice and drop off at the shore. I could have easily fallen in and resurfaced under the ice. Chances are, a group of middle elementary kids would have struggled figuring out an ice rescue. As I scrambled back onto the ice to the laughter of the kids, I was keenly aware that I was very lucky. It was more than luck, but at that point, I only understood luck and not the truth that I had been protected.

On some deep level though, I felt something had been on my side, even though I didn't know what it was or who it was. I didn't yet understand the Heavenly Father's love and plan. Isn't it reassuring to know that God doesn't wait to love and care for us until we know who He is? If we will recognize it, we can look back and realize He sees us and is intricately involved in our lives no matter where we are. David pondered, "Where can I go from your presence"? Whether we admit or not, the answer is nowhere. I get there are other moments of past pain we may not understand. We will come back to that issue later, but for now, let your mind wander to moments you thought you were lucky in your life and spared some type of harm. At second glance, maybe it wasn't luck after all.

As an adult, my clearest recollection of protection was on a mission trip to Zambia, a country located in the southern half of Africa. As part of the itinerary, our team leader had scheduled a specific day for us to cross the Zambezi River by ferry on our way to Botswana. At the last minute the trip was moved up a day earlier. We went on our day trip and returned to Zambia none the wiser that we had been protected. The following day, at the time we would have been on the ferry had we kept our original schedule, a truck overloaded with cobalt caused the ferry to capsize and a number of people drowned or were eaten by crocodiles. As the news spread throughout the nation, we found out about this tragedy. There was a somber realization that had we not changed our itinerary; we would be been part of that disaster. I understood that my life was not of greater value than any of those who perished, but for reasons not understood by me, our team was spared, and my life was spared. It wasn't luck or happenstance. It was God. Although I am not able to tell you the length of each life or each one's specific purpose, I trust the One who does. I had been protected yet was sobered by the reality that others didn't make it. Being grateful for one's life without falling into the trap of feeling more deserving than others is vital in recognizing His protection.

It would be impossible for me to remember the number of times I was knowingly protected. Who knows how many times I was unknowingly protected? But I was, nonetheless. And so, too, have you. Granted, we haven't been spared every struggle, pain, or tragedy; yet, you are here today because you have been protected more times than you know for purposes specifically designed for you by God. I don't have the answers as to why some people's lives are shorter or longer than others. All of us are of the same value to God, but not all of us have the same purpose. The pages were put in place, and it is by more than luck or happenstance that you are here right now.

Right Place, Right Time

God has declared things in His destiny for you, whether you recognize it or not. He put you in the right place at the right time and did so in a way that you couldn't have possibly manufactured it through your own ability. This realization happens throughout your life, but too often we chalk it up to good fortune or karma. People dismiss the Lord out of hand and miss the opportunity to sit in wonder at the movement His powerful hand. He moves both behind the scenes and out in the open to guide and position you according to His plans and purposes.

The year 1994 was one of those times that stands out to me. I was the twenty-four-year-old pastor of a small church in Alexandria, Virginia. As a way of building connection and relationship with our community, I had the idea of doing a special service that would honor our police officers. As far as I knew at the time, no other church was doing this; so, I made contact with our local chief of police. After working through the process and planning, it ended up not coming together. It turns out that the police officers had, unknowingly, already accepted an offer of this type from another church in the area. The chief of police was a gracious man; and as a kind gesture, he invited me to attend a special gathering of law enforcement and city representatives from around the nation to a gathering at the White House. I was flattered at his invitation and accepted this chance to do something I had never done before. As far as I was concerned, it would be a great memory. My vision was short-sighted.

In what seemed to be unrelated to this invitation, something was going on with the church at the same time. The district our church was part of had been assigned a special missions project by our denomination's headquarters. We were to work on establishing a mission work in Albania, and I was considering going on a two-week trip that summer. This small nation in Southern Europe had only gained its freedom from communism four years earlier. I was intrigued and felt the pull to go on the upcoming trip. I had been wondering how we would build connections and relationships and have a positive presence for Christ in the nation. There was also the task of gaining government permission to register our church there and allow for a long-term presence and work to happen.

At this point, the two stories seem completely unrelated. But then God revealed how the two were inextricably connected. The day for the law enforcement gathering came, and I was sitting among hundreds of dignitaries and officials on the White House lawn, just an anonymous guy in the midst of people who were known. I was honored to just be there and sit in my chair. But then I heard a voice from down the row say he was from Albania. Albania? Who would be here from Albania, let alone at an invitation-only White House event? I waited for his conversation to end and then approached to introduce myself. Turns out, this man was the Chief of Staff for the Prime Minister of Albania. The Chief of Police of Alexandria, Virginia, had ancestral roots in Albania and had invited him to be a special guest as well. You may be wondering, like I did, how did the Chief of Police for Alexandria, Virginia, come to meet this leader in the first place? The Albanian Chief of Staff was studying with other leaders at Georgetown University, as part of a special program to train government leaders from the new democracies that emerged at the end of the Cold War. Georgetown University is in Washington D.C., and with Alexandria, Virginia being just across the Potomac River, this proximity was part of the connection.

Of all the countries of the world for our district to be assigned, we were given Albania. Of all the cities in America for me to move to as a pastor, it was Alexandria, Virginia. God made sure the police chief had Albanian roots. God also allowed the idea of the special community service at our church to not come to pass; yet, the Holy Spirit prompted me to have the idea in the first place. When you stop and start pondering all the little details that spanned years that converged for this meeting to take place, it is mind-blowing.

Within the month of this divine appointment, our district leaders were having dinner with the Chief of Staff of the Prime Minister of Albania, learning more of the history and culture of Albania, and warmly being invited to see him when our first team visited Albania. He also offered to introduce us to the governmental official in charge of registering religious groups in the country.

A few months later, I was in Albania's capital, Tirana, watching while our leadership was talking with the man in charge of giving permission for mission groups and churches to be registered in the nation. An older missionary couple had come on the trip to consider giving their final years in ministry to providing leadership for this new work. That meeting with this leader was so remarkable, as God used it to confirm their commitment to move to Albania.

From a human perspective, I may have been the least important person on the White House lawn that day, but God had put together a meeting whose significance dwarfed the pomp and circumstance of the human occasion. It put an indelible mark on my life that God puts us in the right place at the right time, if we will just open our eyes to see, our ears to hear, and our hearts to respond to His amazing plan.

Salvation

On December 24, 1978, I went to live with my dad, stepmom, and brother. Over the previous year and a half, I had been visiting with them a couple weekends a month and a few weeks in the summer. Between the ages four and six, my mother and I had lived in California, while my Dad and brother were thousands of miles away in Georgia or in our family's home state of New Jersey. So, from a child's perspective, I was getting to know my dad, brother, and stepmom for the first time. I had one memory of m‑

dad at five years old but didn't have memories from before that. I know my dad invested much more before we were separated from each other, but my young mind didn't retain it consciously. Now, I was eight, and God was orchestrating events that were drawing me to Him, even though I didn't know it yet.

During the summer and fall of 1978, two key events happened. First, I was sitting in my bedroom, angrily cursing about something that made me mad. That may sound odd, but I had been hanging around the wrong group and had already been cursing like a sailor for a while. I had also been a thief and had stolen many things from a local convenience store (They were called "five-and-dimes" back then). In addition, I had been exposed to a pretty strong dose of pornography through a neighborhood kid who knew where his dad's stash of *Playboys* were. In other words, I had been hanging out with kids who swore, stole, and looked at pornography. Not exactly what any parent would want for their eight-year-old. Thus, the idea of me sitting in my room letting out four-letter words wasn't odd, but on this day, something strange happened. In the midst of the profanity, I felt a presence in my room, who I would later understand to be the Holy Spirit. I heard a voice calmly say that I didn't need to talk like that anymore. And at that moment, the desire to curse stopped just like that.

The second event was in September, when I approached my mother and asked to go live with my father. Please take into account that I was eight years old. I felt the nerve and courage to do this, and it was a courage that was unfamiliar to me. Although she said no, she and my father began a private dialogue about their custody agreement, and what they thought was best for me. On December 23rd a new arrangement was agreed upon by the two of them. I was told I would be going to live with my dad, stepmom, and brother. I packed my stuff; my head swirled with the surprise of it all. On December 24th, at 8:00 p.m., in the parking lot of Ponzio's Diner (New Jersey has lots of diners.), the exchange was made. All of this was part of God drawing me to Himself, even though I didn't understand the eternal implications.

After moving in with them, I started going with my stepmom and brother to church. My brother had asked to go to church some months earlier, and he was one of God's instrument to lead our family toward a personal, saving relationship with Jesus Christ. On Father's Day 1979, my stepmom became a Christian. As

I watched her pray at the altar, my heart began to feel God's tug like never before. One week later, my brother became a Christian. And then, three days later, I was watching Billy Graham on TV on a Wednesday evening. I liked watching TV and was glued to it, listening to Billy Graham as he preached. When the invitation was given, my heart pounded and ached for Jesus. I knew I needed Him. When I asked my stepmom to pray with me, she did. I felt His peace and presence wash over me. That moment has marked my life to this day. June 20, 1979 was the culmination of the work that God had been doing from eternity to draw me to salvation. I was grateful to receive His gift. And here is the great news! I am not loved more by God than anyone else on planet earth. He is working and moving to bring people to Him. If you know Him personally, think back to how He saved you. If you don't know Him yet, He is moving behind the scenes and out in the open because He loves you and wants you to know Him now, and for eternity.

Calling

It was December of 1984, and we were living in Colorado Springs, Colorado. My dad was studying to be a pastor at Nazarene Bible College, and we were attending a Nazarene church called Trinity. Our family's life had been on a whirlwind transformation. In the summer of 1980, my dad had become a Christian. By this point, my stepmom had become Mom to me, and our family was now walking in our first steps of ministry. Dad and Mom were leading the singles' group at church. In addition, we went with two other families to do a worship service at a local retirement/nursing home on Sunday afternoons.

Being around ministry and seeing my dad go to college to be a pastor made me wonder about it personally. I initially chose a path of resistance. Becoming a pastor just because my dad did wasn't what I wanted to do. His example could inspire me, but I thought each person must have their own calling from God on what He wanted their life to be. I was a talker, so at that point, becoming an attorney sounded like a good plan. Of course, becoming an attorney was second to being a professional baseball player like my great-grandfather was, but practicing law seemed like a good fallback plan. It all made sense to me at the ripe old age of fourteen. All of that changed between Christmas and New Year of 1984.

Our teen group went on a winter retreat to Golden Bell Camp-ground in Divide, Colorado. One evening the speaker talked about not being too young to surrender your life to God. He also talked about hearing God's call. My heart was pounding. I was trying not to give in while experiencing the pull of the Holy Spirit to my destiny in Him. When the invitation was given, teens went up to surrender their lives to Christ or to make a deeper commitment in some area of calling. I gripped the seatback of the chair in front of me and kept my head down. Inside my head, I kept saying, "I don't need to go up there." And then I heard a voice say, "You need to go up there." Thinking it was someone talking to me, I turned to look at row behind me to see who was speaking. No one was there. I got up, went forward, knelt with tears, and surrendered my life to a call to ministry as a pastor. It was one month shy of my fifteenth birthday. Once I submitted to His plan, a supernatural peace filled my life, and I was able to share with others that evening of the calling God has placed on my life.

Less than two months later, our youth group was leading the Sunday night service, and I had been given permission to preach the sermon. In a church with many men and women studying for the ministry, the line was long with those who wanted to preach. Now, at fifteen, I stood before 150-200 people and preached my first sermon. My wife, who was then a teen in the same church, has an old cassette tape of that evening.

When I finished preaching, I knew it wasn't a great message. But when the youth pastor gave an invitation to prayer as a response to the message, many came to the front of the sanctuary to pray. I stood there dumbfounded, wondering how they could have responded to that message. I remember standing there, as if I was looking down at myself from above. That moment seemed frozen in time. The Holy Spirit spoke into my spirit, "Remember Kevin, it's always about Me." And that is so true. People weren't kneeling in prayer because of me. The same Holy Spirit who called me was calling them to a closer relationship with Him. It is the same Spirit of God who resides with us today in our world. He is always moving, speaking, guiding, and supernaturally moving. On that night, people were responding to Him, and God wanted me to keep that at the core of my being and calling.

The impact of that truth hasn't waned over the years, even though I haven't always applied it perfectly. There have been seasons of effective ministry, tremendous marriage and family life, and great times of fulfillment in following His calling. There have also been personal distractions, pride, and sin in the years since that night. One thing has been unmistakably true: God has remained faithful. It is always about Him. The same is true for your life. Whatever your calling and whatever His purpose for your life, you would be well served to daily remember the powerful, life-altering truth, "It's always about Him."

Marriage

Does God really care who you marry? I have had some tell me that they don't believe God has a specific person that is His best for you. They see it as a banquet table from which you make your choices. I believe God has a specific plan for each person's life, and in my case, He was gracious enough to be crystal clear with me about who I was supposed to marry. The clear work of His hand has helped Barb and I since our wedding in 1989 make it through when life and marriage wasn't always easy. In fact, we have walked through some roads that have ended many marriages. I believe the strong hand of God that brought us together was the foundation that empowered us to weather some big storms. Here is our story.

We were a fourteen-year-old and fifteen-year-old in our youth group. With large, brown, plastic glasses frames, braces, corduroy pants, and a plaid shirt, I was quite the looker. Barb, on the other hand, was a cute as a button, with dimples and a smile that attracted and disarmed people then, just as it does today. She was easily noticed, though somewhat shy. She was way out of my league for sure. She remembers the day when she noticed me walking into the church and had the thought that she liked me. Thank you, God, for that assist. Well, we were youth group sweethearts for a few months, but then my family moved back to New Jersey for my dad to plant a new church with a church organization we had joined, the Wesleyan Church. The new church was to be in the county surrounding his hometown of Atlantic City, New Jersey. Barb and I were heartbroken as I moved away and tried to keep in touch over the summer, but I didn't understand how things would work.

I now know that when a girl calls you to ask if you want to breakup, she is actually asking for reassurance. Unfortunately, due to my ignorance of the way things really are, I thought she wanted to breakup. Oops! We had very little contact over the next three years as a result of my miscalculation that day. I still thought about her and turns out she thought of me as well. During the summer between my junior and senior year, her friend mailed me Barb's school ID picture, and I carried it in the picture sleeves of my wallet. That was a 1980s reference for those who don't have idea of why people would carry pictures in a wallet. Teens would give and receive wallet-sized prints of the school pictures taken each year.

Why does all this matter? Well, in the fall of 1987, someone stole my wallet. After they took the money, they must have tossed it away. Someone found it, and the only thing left in the wallet was the picture sleeve, and the only identifiable address was on Barb's school I.D. picture. The person who found it put in a small box and mailed it to her school. Barb was called down to the office and received a small box with my wallet in it. She knew it was mine as soon as she saw her picture. (Turns out, she had told her friend to mail it to me).

She called me and we talked on the phone. The reconnecting had begun. A few months later, on my eighteenth birthday, she called, and to my surprise, my dad offered me a high school graduation present while I was on the phone with Barb. He offered me a round-trip plane ticket to see her in Colorado Springs. In the spring of 1988, I flew to Colorado Springs. At this time, you could meet people at the arrival gate. When people walked off the jet way into the terminal, they would scan the people gathered at the gate to find who was there to meet them. As I walked up the jetway, I was looking for Barb, wondering if we would recognize each other right away, since it had been three years. When I saw her, two things inside me clicked. First, I thought she was beautiful, and second, I knew that we would get married one day. This wasn't something shared with her at that moment, as I didn't want her to run screaming out of the airport.

Within a few months, we started dating long distance, racking up large phone bills and writing page upon page of letters. Yes, before texting, email, and social media, people wrote letters. Barb still has all our letters. To my great joy, we were engaged on August 6, 1988, and on June 10, 1989, we were married in the same church we had attended together years earlier. God used a stolen wallet to write on my pages the great gift of a priceless wife who would stand with me through all the ups and downs of life. I am grateful for the handwriting of God on our lives and am thankful He worked real hard to make sure I recognized it.

His Leading and Our Journey of Practicing

Michael Jr. is a fantastic comedian who loves the Lord. I heard him in person at a pastor and wife's conference hosted by the Wesleyan Church (the organization that ordained me). During his routine, he talked about how God walks us through experiences, challenges, and opportunities in life that end up developing the skills, understanding, and values we will need down the road. He referred to it as "practicing without knowing you are practicing." Michael Jr. is right on target. We can't always see this at the moment, and frankly, we don't always want to see it. When we are on top of the world, we tend to want to bask in the glow of it all and take credit. When we go through pain and suffering, we tend to blame God and question His character and love. We can even wrongly conclude that God is indifferent, distant, or sadistic. He is the opposite of all of these, but human suffering can cloud or color our ability to see the Eternal in the midst of the present. God is lovingly marking our lives with His fingerprints, even though we slap His hand away at times. Maybe you have never done this, but I know I have. Sadly, there have been times I was angry at Him for not doing things how and when I wanted them.

Like when I was twenty-six, and God walked me through a forty days of prayer and fasting, in which I drank liquids and one day's worth of solid food during the forty days. It was truly a miraculous time of His power through His Spirit in my life. Throughout the time, I envisioned revival in the church coming, our own Pentecost, so to speak. When the fast was over, it didn't happen. Instead, I was viewed as odd by some and criticized by some in the church where I was the pastor. It was disillusioning. Some were becoming embarrassed at their strange pastor. Unfortunately, I chose to become bitter over not seeing my miraculous daydreams come true. I closed off a part of me to Him because of a sense of failure and wondering why God wouldn't answer my prayers. Clearly, I had much to learn.

But, through fasting in prayer, He did lead me to Colorado two years later. It would take many more years for me to the practice of fasting and let God break through my deep bitterness to teach me how He uses this spiritual discipline in our walk with Him. Fasting draws us closer to Him and releases the power of His Holy Spirit in us and through us for the Father's glory. It's not about my personal agenda, no matter how good it may seem to me.

What I am trying to illustrate is that my life was marked by the dueling perspectives of my heart. I genuinely chased after God and His kingdom but also grappled with an unhealthy yearning for selfish ambition to meet my inner needs, assuage lifelong pain and feelings of rejection. I was stuck in a place where I needed healing from past pain and present moments of embarrassment. In spite of all this, God was faithful and continued to draw me closer to Him. He knew my heart wanted more of Him, just as He knew there were glaring weaknesses and unhealed wounds. I am grateful God loves us enough to continue to draw us to Himself, in spite of ourselves. It is who He is. He sees in each of us what we don't always see in ourselves. My heart hungered for God while I still wrestled with the hurts of my heart.

I can think of a worship rally my church and I attended with other churches in 1994. As the denominational leader spoke of the heart cry for revival in our land, he challenged us to ask God to start the revival inside a circle we drew, with us in the middle of the circle. I wept at the invitation to prayer, yearning for more of Him. Throughout the years, I would have several of these moments, with long periods of the journey in between. God worked through both, leading me to a place of surrender to Him and total reliance on His supernatural power to do what I could never do. Still, the hunger and the hurts battled inside of me well into my forties. After years of struggle, I experienced a breakthrough of His love that overcame my hurts, both self-inflicted, and done by others.

In October of 2015, I was wracked with a secret-sin struggle that ultimately led to me taking a break from ministry in June of 2016. Desperate for the conflict and contradiction of my life to end, God reached out to me beyond my ability to even ask. He overwhelmed me with a deeper indwelling of His Holy Spirit beyond what I had ever experienced or known. Something inside me radically changed that evening. A deep struggle was over. The healing of wounds was miraculous. His power stunned me that night. I will never be the same, and I praise the Lord for that. Marriage, parenting, ministry, and all of life is supernaturally different because of the Spirit of God and the authority of Jesus Christ.

The compromises and sin prior to that night would still require an accountability, but God radically changed me. God had been growing my heart's desire for Him to the point that all other wrong desires were overcome by His power. Did it take too long for me to see this and surrender to it? Absolutely. But God was still faithful to have me practicing the right things even as I struggled with the wrong. He is amazing beyond description and loves us beyond measure.

Maybe you identify with the description of pain you can't heal, a past you can't escape, or glory days you can't re-create. Instead of shaking your fist at the sky, I invite you to stop and ask, "What might God be having you practice as part of His plan as opposed to clinging to your own practices"? If you are practicing the coping mechanisms and mindsets that are not from God, it will lead to brokenness and bondage in many forms. God's plan and practices, on the other hand, lead to healing and freedom unlike anything a person can accomplish on his or her own.

Maybe you feel like you have gone too far for God to bring you back. You might believe the pages of your book are stuck and you keep reliving the same cycle of pain and disappointment. God is the One who can redeem your life and the time of your days. He can flutter the pages forward and fulfill all He has written for you in His books. Inside the title page of books is the copyright page and © is the symbol you see to inform you that the author retains all rights on what He has written. Well, the Father wrote about your life before time began, and Jesus Christ is our © that tells us that His death and resurrection has the full authority over everything that has separated you from Him prior to salvation or a struggle that still enslaves you today as a Christ follower. The Holy Spirit wants to do and can do for you what you could never do for yourself.

***

I urge you to stop buying the lie that it is too late or that your life is some random game of chance. He has a book just for you. As you have just read examples from my story, reflect on your own. He can heal the pain no one else can. He can bring His plan to pass even when you believe you missed key moments in the past. He can help you look to His glory instead of trying to relive your past glory days.

When you sin, or have been cast aside by others, God wants to make you a son or daughter in His family. He can resolve the accusations of the enemy against your life. He wants you to live out His destined plan for your life. And He has the power to bring to pass the story He has written for you.

Chapter Four
It's a Wonderful Life, But Only if You See It

L ike many homes, we have traditions that remind us it is Christmas. On Christmas Eve, we go to church and then have chocolate and cheese fondues and all the accoutrements (fancy word for fixings) that go with it. The kids get to unwrap one gift, picked out by Mom. Usually it's the pajamas they wear that night into Christmas morning. In regard to food, the kids look forward to Friendship Tea, Overnight Fondue (egg casserole), and Christmas brunch (with bacon that has been basted with maple syrup). On Christmas morning, there is the reading of the Christmas story, minus the genealogies. My wife gives out the presents and takes pictures. Then she cleans up all the wrapping paper while I help with the brunch. Later, there are the phone calls to out-of-state relatives to say thank you for the gifts and wish them a Merry Christmas.

Later in the day, there is a ham or turkey dinner, even though folks are still somewhat full from brunch. We eat candy and snacks throughout the day, and in the evening, we usually relax with a movie. It is a great day. I imagine many of you can recall your own Christmas traditions as well.

There is another tradition that is very special to me. Sometime during the Christmas season, I watch *It's A Wonderful Life*. It is the black-and-white Frank Capra movie from 1946. It was Jimmy Stewart's first movie after World War II, and it is one of many Christmas movies that families watch each year. Some watch *A Christmas Story*, reliving the adventures of Ralphie and his Red Ryder BB gun, but for me, it's all about *It's A Wonderful Life* and the main character, George Bailey. If you have never watched this movie, let

35

me give you a thumbnail sketch of this holiday classic.

George Bailey is the man who wants out of his childhood home of Bedford Falls for the life he dreamed about for years. He wants to be a world traveler, architect of skyscrapers, and pursuer of all the glory he can imagine. Unfortunately for George, reality is an unyielding ball and chain on his dreams. His father dies when he is eighteen, leaving George left to run the perpetually struggling Bailey Brother's Savings and Loan. He puts his younger brother, Harry, through college instead of going himself. Harry goes on to achieve success in college athletics, romance, and wins the Congressional Medal of Honor in World War II as a fighter pilot.

Harry looks the part of the dashing hero, and George looks the part of the guy who just can't catch a break. George loves his brother and is proud of him. In spite of the heartfelt joy over Harry's successes, George is quietly embittered that life is passing him by. By twenty-six, George is working hard but missing the life he could have because he is dreaming of the life he doesn't have. He marries the woman who has always unconditionally loved him (Mary), has four kids, and weathers the storms of life. All the while, George grows more bitter and resentful. He has a wife who loves him, four kids who adore him, and has a town who sees his work as irreplaceable. All this is nothing compared to the cauldron of bitterness and anger over his financial struggles and business challenges. He feels trapped by the expectations of others and his own sense of duty and responsibility.

As he reaches the pivotal crisis point of his life, George acquaints an angel assigned to help him in his moment of deepest need. George doesn't see this as divine intervention when he meets his not-so-impressive angel named Clarence. Clarence offers George the chance to see what the world would look like if he had never been born. Clarence declares it so, and they begin to experience Bedford Falls as if George Bailey never existed.

George doesn't believe what Clarence is telling him, but he keeps interacting with people who don't know him but should. He is horrified to see how heartless and hopeless Bedford Falls had become, but Clarence informs him that this is what Bedford Falls became because George wasn't there to be all that he was created to be. His wife doesn't know him, his kids were never born, and his brother, Harry, died as a child because George wasn't there to save him from drowning.

The movie crescendos with George begging God to let him live again, demonstrating his salvation moment with God. It begins to snow, and George finds out he is back in Bedford Falls as he knows it. Suddenly all the things that he saw as problems and burdens were now his blessings. He runs through Bedford Falls in exuberant joy. His wife loves him, and his friends come to the rescue and give back to George after all the years he gave to them. It is a great ending. I admit it is a sappy Hollywood feel-good movie. I watch it every year and cry and laugh at the same places. I can quote most of the movie. It is a great Christmas tradition. Yet, for a number of years, I resonated more with the bitter George Bailey than the grateful one. I wanted to connect with George at the end of the movie, but I didn't once the warm fuzzy of the movie wore off.

I didn't let the lessons about gratitude, contentment, and counting one's blessings go deep enough into my being to change my perspective. And that is the point. We can watch, read, and listen to the good stuff but not learn the lessons attached to it. It is a "Wonderful Life," but only if you see it. Without a proper, God-centered perspective, you and I can fall into the pit of despair. Entitlement, bitterness, self-pity, anger, hatred, and more can entangle and entrap our lives. For almost a quarter of a century, I preached about this, gave advice on it, and pointed people to viewing life through God's lens. But there was a level I didn't let penetrate into the deep places of my life. How did this happen?

It started with seeing the glass as half empty as I pursued success. In college I played soccer on a partial scholarship. For three years I worked and worked to become the top goalie on the team. I fell short. I didn't play my senior year so that I could focus on preparation for ministry and was the interim pastor of a nearby church, but I carried bitterness because I didn't think I got a fair shake. Was it true? Doesn't matter. I missed the fact that a top-flight education that cost $50,000 twenty-five years ago was 85% paid for so that my family and I weren't saddled with crippling student loan debt. I missed the fact that I was privileged to play, and many would have traded spots with me. I focused more on what I felt I missed out on rather than what I had received.

This problem continued over the years in other skewed mindsets. An older pastor complimented me when I was twenty-two and said I would become a national leader in our denomination one day. Rather than taking it as a compliment to encourage me, I took it as a goal to be pursued, to the point that I was frustrated when I didn't advance quicker in leadership opportunities at the regional level or see more church growth at the local level. Sound repulsive and self-centered? It was.

When Barb and I were busy with raising our four kids, there were times I thought she saw me as a paycheck who did tasks around the house. I believed I was an obligation to her, not one she loved just because she loved me. Was all this true? Of course not. But I had been carrying a skewed perspective on how others viewed me since the early years of my life. My belief was that if I didn't perform or live up to expectations, people would reject me and cast me aside. Granted, some did act this way, but my wife and kids never did, even though I thought they would. I believed I was disposable and of little value. I yearned to be important, successful, and admired. Besides my perspective being skewed, I also had a pronoun problem. They were called "I" and "my."

So I nursed my wounds and fought with my bitterness. In time, it turned into entitlement. The time came when I became blinded by it and hurt many people through selfish, sinful behavior. A woman came along who began to compliment me, listen to me, and want emotional connection with me. She was in a broken place and so was I, but I, as the pastor, was held to a higher standard and never should have crossed the boundaries that I did.

The red flags were there. There were men in my life for personal accountability, and I chose to hide my struggle from them. I rationalized the emotional bond with her, and it left my wife, Barb, feeling wounded, alone, and betrayed. I was close friends with the woman's husband, and I inexcusably betrayed and hurt him. Instead of a moment of revelation on a snowy bridge, I got the consequences of real life. I crossed some physical boundaries, tried to conceal it and move on, and was foolish in my assumptions. I was truly repentant, but somehow believed I could avoid the human consequences. God had forgiven me, but the domino effect of my failure as a spiritual leader had to be addressed. Eight months after I had stopped the inappropriate relationship, someone contacted the office of my regional director to report my sin. The failure was only amplified by the fact that my wife was the office manager for our region and received the email detailing this failure and sin. She was hurt in ways no wife ever deserves to be hurt.

What followed was me resigning from my job, having to tell

38

my four kids what happened, as well as several dozen others who were board members, friends, accountability partners, family members, and authorities in my life. The public statement at my resignation was a truthful account of the severe burnout I had been having the last couple of years and how I needed to step away from ministry. The details were reserved for a smaller number. Until now.

As I watched my wife, kids, and hundreds of others impacted by my sin and failure, it was like watching a fire burn out of control with no ability to stop it. The closest Biblical example I related to was when David had sinned, and the nation was paying the price with thousands dying because of his personal failure and sin. He begged God to let him pay the price, saying they were sheep and innocent of wrongdoing. The former shepherd had failed in his responsibility as a shepherd, and he agonized that others were paying the price for it. I may not be David, but I understood the horror of seeing others hurt because of my sin.

You see, I ultimately had an epiphany like George Bailey, but the people around me didn't get a neat and tidy Hollywood ending. The lies I had believed about my perceived worthlessness and disposability came crashing down as I saw that my life was more interconnected that I had fathomed. The ripple effect of my actions impacted so many. I didn't see what the world would be like if I had never existed. I saw what happened when I chose selfishness and sin and how my seemingly disposable life touched more than I imagined. In the midst of it, God's redemption and grace was revealed in a way that surprised me, but others shouldn't have been hurt for me to see it.

As I walked through the process of confessing my sin and admitting what I had done, many people began to show me grace and forgiveness when I was expecting the torches and pitchforks. Oh, there were many hard conversations, and repentance with God and others happened on many occasions. Dozens of hard conversations revealed the hurt and disappointment I had caused. But there was far less condemnation that I expected. Instead, there was forgiveness and an unrelenting message that people still saw me as man of God and had complete confidence that my greatest days in the Lord were yet to come. Although time and distance faded most of those relationships, it wasn't done to punish. People move on as they are supposed to, but most gave redemptive words and actions before they did.

For all the times the church gets accused of shooting its wounded, that isn't what happened to me. It was a surprising gift I didn't deserve but am grateful I received. Trying to explain it as people paying me back for years of hard work just didn't jive with the reality of what I was experiencing. It was only explained as a move of the Holy Spirit in people's lives to see me as God saw me. It was grace and mercy like I had preached but didn't believe was for me. When I resigned, it had been eight months since God had broken me and filled me with His Holy Spirit as never before. I had tried to live in the new power while running from the past. When it ended, His presence and power remained, even if my position of leadership in the church ended for a period of time.

Now He was manifesting a change in me by showing me how some still saw me through His eyes. I never should have concealed the secret of my sin and tried to carry it privately out of fear of losing everything. Nor was it right to believe it was loving to keep everyone in the dark, especially Barb, to protect them from hurt. The secrecy caused its own pain. Now, with the truth in the open, I saw the folly of my bitterness, but I also saw the amazing grace of God shown through His Spirit and many of His people.

No, I didn't get to run through the streets of Bedford Falls as the Christmas snow fell and hear everyone sing "Hark the Herald Angels Sing." There is a journey to restoration, and it is paved with accountability and truth. It isn't for me to tell people when they can trust me again. Each must make their own decision. Healing and wholeness have their own clock.

But I realized I was more blessed than I previously understood. In my past bitterness, I missed all my blessings. Now, with the bitterness washed away, I saw clearly. Whatever complaints I had about my wife were minor and fell to the wayside as I saw the grace she showed and the love she had for me all along. She shouldn't have had to go through such a torturous betrayal for me to get a clue. My children forgave me and still looked up to me as their father with respect. They shouldn't have had to demonstrate this through listening to me confess my sin to them. Many friends, colleagues, parents, and family responded the same way. They shouldn't have had their trust broken for me to realize how they saw me.

40

Here's the point. They already saw me in I way that I didn't see myself. Just because I didn't see it doesn't mean they did something wrong. The change of perspective had to happen in me. Remember what God told Jeremiah, "If you take out the precious from the vile, you shall be as my mouth" (Jeremiah 15:19). When the vile poison of bitterness is sifted out, the precious is seen more clearly. George Bailey was blessed all along and so was I. Does this mean life is perfect? No. Does it mean that relationships aren't work? No. It does mean that many of our lives are more blessed than we think or are willing to see.

As you think about where you are, I urge you to be careful regarding infection of bitterness. It is a sin and mindset that will blur your thinking to the point that you will sabotage your life and hurt others in the attempt to find a life you may already have. It will lead you to react to the hurts and wounds you have experienced by becoming one who wounds others blindly and badly. The victim becomes the victimizer. Whether it is chasing the glory days, feeling as though life has been a series of missed opportunities, or being trapped by past pain, unaddressed bitterness robs us of seeing our blessings.

God speaks with clarity in His Word about avoiding bitterness. Look at these examples:

> *And do not grieve the Holy Spirit of God, by whom you were sealed for the day of redemption. Let all bitterness, wrath, anger, clamor, and evil speaking be put away from you, with all malice. And be kind to one another, tenderhearted, forgiving one another, even as God in Christ forgave you.*

—Ephesians 4:30-32

> *looking carefully lest anyone fall short of the grace of God; lest any root of bitterness springing up cause trouble, and by this many become defiled;*

—Hebrews 12:15

> *For all the law is fulfilled in one word, even in this: "You shall love your neighbor as yourself." But if you bite and devour one another, beware lest you be consumed by one another!*

41

—Galatians 5:14-15

The phrase that "hurting people hurt people" is all too fitting here. God doesn't want you to be dismantled by the trap of bitterness. He wants to heal you. His Holy Spirit wants to indwell and empower you. For many, this revelation is a journey. The problem is, if you are trapped by bitterness, you get off on the wrong road. It is a horrific detour. So much of the good you sincerely do and the character you strive to develop can be damaged by sins that come from believing in and acting out bitterness. Listen to these truths of the Word of God.

Dead flies putrefy the perfumer's ointment,

And cause it to give off a foul odor;

So does a little folly to one respected for wisdom and honor. —Ecclesiastes 10:1

When a righteous man turns away from his righteousness, commits iniquity, and dies in it, it is because of the iniquity which he has done that he dies. Again, when a wicked man turns away from the wickedness which he committed, and does what is lawful and right, he preserves himself alive. Because he considers and turns away from all the transgressions which he committed, he shall surely live; he shall not die. Yet the house of Israel says, 'The way of the Lord is not fair.' O house of Israel, is it not My ways which are fair, and your ways which are not fair?

"Therefore I will judge you, O house of Israel, every one according to his ways," says the Lord God. "Repent, and turn from all your transgressions, so that iniquity will not be your ruin. Cast away from you all the transgressions which you have committed, and get yourselves a new heart and a new spirit. For why should you die, O house of Israel? For I have no pleasure in the death of one who dies," says the Lord God. "Therefore turn and live!"

—Ezekiel 18:26-32

42

God wants you to live, and He wants you to have freedom in Him. He wants you to be free from the enslaving power of bitterness and the sinful, hurtful behavior that accompanies it. He wants you to be free from self-hatred at one extreme or entitled self-centeredness at the other. He wants you see life as it really is and as it really can be.

It is a "Wonderful Life" but only if you are willing to see it.

Chapter Five

The Games We Play

Sometimes, we don't fully realize how the events of our past affect us. Whether trying to relive the past, make up for the past, or cover the wounds of the past, each of us can compensate without realizing the "why" behind "what" we do. Although there is a myriad of ways this can manifest itself in person's life, this chapter deals with what it looks like when we seek the wrong kind of attention from others. In many cases, the attention seeking of the present is rooted in trying to compensate for something in the past. Ponder this as you read about the games people play.

My wife is a calm, quiet personality that brings a stable, nurturing presence to our home. The children have always felt safe talking to her about whatever is on their minds. Friends and acquaintances are drawn to friendship with her and trust her deeply. People feel better about themselves just being around her. A red flag for me that someone is a difficult person is when they can't get along with Barb. She builds people up and doesn't view life as a competition in which others must be defeated for her to feel victorious. But, despite all these glowing truths about her, there is a dark secret lurking behind the closed doors of our home. Few get to see this amazing woman become transformed into a bloodthirsty warrior out for the ruin of others. What is the culprit for tripping up this Proverbs 31 woman? None other than the game of Risk. Many a righteous person has been caught in the trap of this insidious game of global conquest.

Okay. Okay. I am laying it on thick. But it is true that we change when we play certain games. Maybe in your home it is Monopoly. Could it be card games? Not your thing? Well, maybe some of you have lost large chunks of your life playing Minecraft, the latest Madden football game, the new installment of NBA 2K, or other video games. Hopefully, you aren't dodging traffic, skirting cliffs, and breaking and entering in the pursuit of Pokémon Go. If we aren't careful, playing games change us, and not always for the good. As you can guess, this is not just about board games anymore.

The problem of letting games change us can be tragically true in the relationship games people play with each other. God has given us clear boundaries to protect us from the damaging results of relationship game playing. Many of us ignore them when we are in pursuit of the approval, power, or gratification we desire. The broken places from our past that need redemption can fuel this unhealthy pursuit. We don't often talk about the emotional games in relationships, in part I think, because it is something we quietly allow because it seems to meet a need for those involved in it.

Peel back the curtain, and I believe you will see that much of the brokenness in marriages, families, and individuals comes from the consequences of these games. Unfortunately, there are dark, destructive places we can end up in if we play long enough. Some of the evil and sin we commit against each other, ourselves, and God began with games that we saw as harmless compensations for deeper needs that we believed were manageable, as long as we played on our terms. What are these games? Well, although not an exhaustive list, let's take a few moments, pull back the curtain, and put words to the dangerous games used to compensate for lost glory days, past regrets, and lingering pain. This escape can become an enslaving, deceptive trap that perpetuates the pain of the past into the present and impacts one's future as well.

The Game of Looks

Without a word, we can communicate so much. Most wouldn't come out and say, "I am looking for someone to play a game of approval and emotional connection." But we use our looks to troll the waters for attention or affirmation. Both men and women do this. If you were part of a reality TV show, the cameras would pick up the nuance of this game. At first, the cameras would stand out awkwardly, but in time they would become part of the scenery, and people would relax. Here is what they would capture on camera. You look just a little bit longer into someone's eyes, a little more deeply than you should. The smile is bigger than you give your spouse. Your spouse can be a pain in the neck and sure doesn't appreciate you. The other person laughs really hard at your jokes, smiles in a way that brightens your day, and looks at you in a way that pierces deeply into your being. As you pay too much attention, you notice facial expressions and body language and become very attentive. The furrowed brow or frown causes you to check and see if everything is okay. You look for reasons to make eye contact. It looks like friendliness to everyone else, but you are getting needs met from this person that should be only reserved for a spouse. As the cameras shift, they reveal another type of player in this game.

Maybe you aren't the monogamist looker but are just a flirt. You will exchange smiles, winked eyes, and bright faces with anyone who will respond. There may be no depth to it, but you are playing games and using people to feel attractive, liked, and popular. You really don't care for others as much as they think, but you want to receive their affirmation. Your influence with looks is for personal gain, manipulation, and ego boosts. Your spouse, kids, friends, and family see it more than you think. Your reputation suffers, and others are strung along as you play your game. This game needs to stop. It is an entryway to deeper problems. If any of us choose denial, defensiveness, or rationalizing when confronted, it isn't convincing to God and sure doesn't fool our family over the long haul. Even those in the periphery of our lives are fooled less than we think.

Game of Words

This one is interesting in that we can disguise it on the front end as being kind to someone. Long before a person is sharing deeply about matters of the heart or frustrations about your spouse, it can begin as compliments and thoughtful conversation. Jokes, stories, and opinions are shared as you look for who responds positively. Your spouse and kids have heard your jokes too many times to find them amusing anymore. They don't realize the gift they have in you (dripping sarcasm), but someone else is listening. And in time, so are you. Like the layers of soil and sediment on the walls of a canyon, the more you dig into a person's life, the price of the depth is a deeper hole for yourself and the other person. Words of appreciation turn to words of care. Words of care turn to words of confiding. Words of confiding turn to words of affection. Words of affection turn to words of commitment. Now you have a big problem, but you weren't willing to see it until you are at the bottom of this canyon of compromise.

If you want to diagnose if you are playing this game, reflect on how you talk to your spouse, kids, and family who aren't meeting your needs as you would like. Does it sound like the way you talk to the person who is giving you attention? If you are affirming someone you shouldn't, there is a good chance you are being critical or distant towards those you are supposed to build up. Another symptom is when you find you don't have the energy or desire to talk when you get home because you have poured yourself into someone else. This isn't about the introvert who is just tired after dealing with people all day and needs to recharge the battery. This is about the person who can't wait to talk to someone else outside the home when he/she should really be reserving that anticipation for their own spouse, kids, or safe friends who are fans of your marriage and family.

Put it this way. Some people can't stand eating leftovers for lunch the next day. Maybe you are one of them. Twice-warmed food just doesn't taste the same. The flavor is lost, the texture is mushy, or the edges are crusty. Leftover lovers like me will tout how lasagna, stew, and soups just keep getting better. Yet, it doesn't work with a Caesar salad or a sandwich slathered with mayo or guacamole. Leftovers represent yesterday's effort passed on to satisfy today's hunger. It may work with some foods, but most will find it wanting when it comes to relationships. If you are giving your home your leftover words and listening, ask yourself who is getting your home-cooked meal?

Some might try and defend their behavior at home by talking about how demanding their job is. This won't fly because there is a difference between a busy day and a distracted life. If busyness is your struggle, then you need to let your day go on the way home from work and get ready for your next investment, which are the people who live in your home. A distracted person, on the other hand, has invested his or her words into someone they shouldn't have. The bond grows deeper and is leading to a crisis. Either you are going to sever ties by wounding the one you never should have bonded with, or you are going to look for ways to sever ties with the one you were supposed to stay bonded with in the first place. Words have power, and they are dangerous when used for games. They have a lingering memory, even though we wish this wasn't so. The Bible wasn't being figurative when it says, "Death and life *are* in the power of the tongue, And those who love it will eat its fruit" (Proverbs 18:21). If I use my speech to give life-giving words, it produces good fruit. If I use my words to speak death into a situation, the harvest will be hard to digest.

Relationships

This game is about definition and boundaries. In a nutshell, here is how to recognize if you are playing the game and how to stop if you are. If you are married, you shouldn't have a close opposite-sex friend who isn't also friends with your spouse. Second, if the opposite-sex friend is also a friend of your spouse, he/she needs to be closer to your spouse than you.

A red flag should be raised if you are closer to the opposite sex friend than your mate. We can throw around the term "work spouse" with humor, but there is real danger with the game of relationships. There may be a small percentage who can keep it all straight and morally right before God and others. But there are many more who end up marginalizing their spouse while connecting too deeply with an opposite-sex friend.

I know some disagree with me on this. Maybe you are reading this and rejecting it out of hand. The question I have is "Why"? Why would it be a problem to make sure you are not putting a common friend above your spouse in terms of time, emotional bonding, and relational investment? If your spouse isn't too closed off or afraid to speak his/her mind, have a private conversation and see if he/she will open up about how the relationship in question really looks to him/her or makes him/her feel. Instead of critiquing their thoughts or trying to poke holes in their perspective, take some time to listen and reflect on how you are impacting your mate.

Sometimes we like games when we are winning or playing by our own set of rules. In other words, this game seems fine when we are one playing it but wrong if someone else is playing it. Be careful on this one. I know from personal experience what it is to fail and do what God hates. Proverbs 6:19 says He hates "one who sows discord among brethren." He hates the behavior that breaks relationships. As one who has done this and saw the destruction caused, I am grateful for God's amazing forgiveness and grace, but that doesn't change the fact that I hurt people. God's goodness doesn't excuse the painful truth that I devastated my wife and others, and displeased and grieved the Holy Spirit. For a time, I hated the consequences of sin more than I hated the sin. All this game does is hurt others in the long run. I never should have played the game, and neither should you.

The Game of Crisis

This is the game of getting attention through pointing out your struggles. The key to this game is that you aren't looking for a solution from others but rather their sympathy. The goal is getting your needs met through conversation and affirmation as you share how tough things are in your life. The other player in the game is the one who gets affirmation or needs met by being the hero of the story and the fixer of another's problems. Ouch. Far too many times as a pastor, I rushed in to fix the problem and was a player in the game of crisis. I mean, if the person has been hard to please, surely my relational skills will make me hero—I mean a pastor, who can make them happy. Looking back, it is amazing how negative people were attracted to having me attempt to solve their problems. Here's the catch though. Most didn't take the solutions, and sometimes I wanted to be the solution. They wanted the attention, and I wanted the intoxicating feeling of being the hero of the story. Big problem! God is always the hero of the story. It was never meant to be about me, just as it was never meant to be about you.

At this point, I need to be clear on something. Most of the people who were part of the churches I served were great people who genuinely wanted to see others transformed and loved by the power of Christ. The problem was that I allowed too many crisis-driven people to have influence in the church. Thus, the spiritually healthy people had to grapple with those who had no business being in leadership. Spiritually healthy people trusted me as a spiritual leader, but I let them down by not having clearer boundaries with crisis-driven people who had no interest in becoming well.

The game of crisis can be with those of the same gender, opposite gender, young or old. If you are working harder on someone else's problems than they are, you might be in the game of crisis. If you can't let others fail but keep rescuing them so that you are the hero, you might be in the game of crisis. If most of your daily problems are usually someone else's fault and you are good at deflecting any personal responsibility, you might be in the game of crisis. If you make sure you are in the role of correcting and teaching others but never seem to allow yourself to be taught or corrected, you might be playing the game of crisis. While it is true that all of us will have real crisis at times, I don't believe we were supposed to live life in perpetual crisis. And we were never supposed to make it a game to meet relational needs.

Appearance

If you find yourself wanting to look good for someone who isn't your spouse, then you are playing the game of appearance. But at the same time, if you are so purposefully casual, or dare I say sloppy, you can be telling someone you know they don't have value to you. So, there can be two types of players in this game—placing value in the wrong person's approval or not showing value to the one you should. Let's look at a couple of scenarios.

If you are a stay-at-home mom or dad who doesn't care enough to make sure that you and the house are kept in some semblance of order, you have taken on the role of the lazy player in the game of appearance. When my wife was on bedrest with our third child, she had to stay in bed or on the couch for twelve weeks. Twice a day she had to send readings of her contractions over the phone/modem connection (old technology of late 1995). Our daughter's life was at stake. In addition to working as a pastor, I cooked, cleaned, and took care of our two kids (five, two and a half). It was an intense three months.

But guess what? I did what had to be done, and so did my wife, and so have countless others when the chips were down. The laundry was done, kids were bathed, meals were cooked, and I still did the work of a pastor. Fortunately, we had a friend in the church who gave invaluable help. But I also had to decide to do my part in taking care of Barb, and she had to choose to be still when she wanted to be active. This isn't meant to elevate us. Barb and I made vows to each other, and she has taken care of me, just as I have helped her. Here's the point. Most of us can get more done on a given day if we just choose to do so. Laziness and procrastination aren't virtues. Don't use the gift of time you have been given as an excuse for sloppy living, only to jump on your spouse to help you when you are mismanaging your life. Before some of you get too irate, let's move on to the next scenario.

Some find it nice to be able to get dressed up and go to work. Oh, they may complain about it, but there is value in working hard toward seeing the goals of an organization come to pass. Any job done well for the glory of God that doesn't violate His laws and commands is a good job. In the midst of a workday though, we can play the game of appearance when we start noticing how nice others look and how good they seem to act and behave at work. We go home to a vomiting child or a busy family schedule and can begin to get critical of our spouse and kids.

If both spouses work, this can add to it because who has enough energy to get the kids fed, pay the bills, clean the house, and attend the extracurricular activities that always seem to be on the schedule? When this stress elevates and criticism toward our spouse escalates, the opposite gender at work starts to look and act better than our spouse at home. This game of appearance starts to seep into how you get ready for work, what you look forward to at work, and how you act at work. The tendency is to give more to those who feed our need of affirmation. It is a dangerous game because we aren't measuring accurately. Our spouse has made sacrifices, and sees us at our worst, while a coworker tends to see us at our best.

A great way to get out of this game is to have a reality check. Remember this key fact. Everyone at work is getting paid to look and act nice. You see an intentional attempt at professionalism because they want to keep their job and get paid. You don't see how most coworkers behave after they get home. You don't see when they decide to have a no-bathing day, let their house get messy, or get to smell their breath first thing in the morning.

My poor wife has spent twenty-seven years being married to a man who used to sound like Darth Vader when he slept. My morning breath could have killed small animals. Only after God instantaneously healed my asthma in 2016 did it get better. Barb sees me at my worst, while others tend to see me at my best. One could argue that we also get to see each other authentically, with all the positive that comes with it as well. Very true. The reality check isn't meant to minimize the positives at home but rather temper the idealism at work. When someone is paid to look good and act good, it isn't the same as the one who has chosen to commit their life to be with you for better or worse. We need to clean up for each other often enough to communicate value, while also rejecting the game of appearance with those at work.

Touch

"I am a hugger." That was my line. But somehow, I hugged others more than my own wife. This game is based in presuming others will operate within our "bubble," rather than being aware of theirs. There are genuinely innocent huggers who just love people, but all need to be careful about the game of touch. It can be the hand on the arm, a playful nudge, or the brush of the hand as you walk past. When you cross the touch barrier without innocent motives, it is a game of risk that can have real consequences. For years, I would work the room as the gregarious extrovert, shaking hands, hugging, and fist bumping, and just being a fun-loving guy. But under the surface, I noticed when a woman got more out of a hug than she should have, or vice versa, when I did. I spent too much time paying attention to others. Barb told me one day that she felt like a single woman when she was at church. Wow! That was an epic failure on my part, and it led to a change.

After too many years of wounding her heart as I doted on others, two practices began. First, she would stand with me when I greeted others. Second, I would only hug those who initiated a hug with me. Other than that, it was all handshakes. Funny thing happened. Some people stopped coming up to greet me once Barb was standing next to me. Interesting. As for me waiting for others to initiate a hug, 80-90 percent of the men and women I hugged never initiated a hug once I stopped. There were quite happy to just shake hands, and to admit it, I was quite surprised.

Think about it. For years, I was invading people's space and they were just being polite. This was a humbling lesson and thank God for it. There were also unexpected positives I noticed once I had healthier physical boundaries. It was a joy when a grandma and grandpa brought their two grandkids to me each week for me to kneel and greet them. By not looking to move through the crowd, the interactions God had in mind were more special. It became more about others and the divine appointments God had in mind.

One more thing about touch. When you cross lines, you get used to them, then you are vulnerable to cross new lines when it comes to the opposite sex. A touch can become a hug. A hug becomes an embrace. An embrace becomes a kiss. A kiss becomes passionate kissing. Passionate kissing becomes foreplay. And foreplay becomes sex. Teaching our teens and single young adults to have strong boundaries with physical/sexual expressions is because you can only go so far before you go all the way. There are many married men and women who have fallen into adulterous sins they never thought could happen, and there are many single people who ended up in bed with someone unexpectedly.

There are too many teens and young adults who become pregnant, contract STDs, abort a child, or face the trauma of post-abortion issues because they experiment with the game of touch beyond where they should or are ready for. Is touch some disease to be avoided? Of course not. It is a powerful expression of affirmation and love that needs to be wisely and virtuously shared with the right people at the right time.

Social Media

Between FaceTime, Snapchat, Instagram, Messenger, Facebook, texting, and other applications, the written word and visual interaction can be communicated in real time. We see third-world citizens brought into the global culture through these technologies. Dictatorships have been toppled. Families and friends are connected around the globe. Business, education, and medicine have been advanced. There are many uses that have made our world a better place. But we also have seen many uses that have made our world a worse place. Pornography and human trafficking have grown exponentially into a global epidemic. The sex trade exploits women and children, as well as some men and cost many their lives. These poisons use various social media platforms as connection points to spread this disease of sin and slavery. When it comes to the games people play in inappropriate relationships, the practice of inappropriate and sexual communication through all these social media platforms and applications has become prevalent. Seemingly innocent connections can turn the "game" into a wasteland of destruction.

Here's the point. Social media must be carefully filtered and used with clear boundaries. I urge you to consider giving passwords from all your social media/email accounts to your spouse. Unless limited by a top-secret clearance or mandatory confidentiality in your profession, give complete access and passwords for your cellphone, email, and social media to your spouse, and vice versa. If everyone knows your spouse will see what it is said and done, it will protect you both. To those who feel like it treats them like a child, try looking at it this way. Your employer can retain the right to see every digital and video communication done with their equipment. You allow this accountability from your boss. Why not commit to you and your spouse protecting each other? For those who bristle at this as childish and unnecessary, I do understand. I just don't agree. I took that defensive posture for a time, and it almost ruined my marriage and family. It was too easy to have a rationalized compromise. Be smart before you fall, not just after you fall.

Stepping-Stones

The last game being highlighted in this chapter is the game of using people as stepping-stones in relationships. In simpler versions, we see this play out in junior high and high schools. If you are popular and decide to like me, then I am popular because of your endorsement and approval. Students end up dividing into groups of varying levels of social acceptance. Unfortunately, this doesn't stop for everyone when they become adults. People see someone who has something, is something, or has influence with someone. By getting their endorsement, it gives a type of credibility and recognition, even if temporary.

This doesn't mean that all approval is harmful. There are healthy expressions of gaining approval. We want our doctors to have passed all their classes, internships, and residencies. Many occupations have apprentice relationships that are utilized to gain skill and training. We want children and adults alike to respect authority in their lives. The negative expression I am talking about is seeing people as disposable and as a resource to be used. This is a realm of manipulation and self-serving attitudes.

If you do something for me, I will connect in relationship until I am tired of you, have you need me/meet my needs, feel guilty for my ethical contradiction, or move on to someone else. People do this in individual relationships, families, groups we belong to, companies we work for, and even churches we attend. It would always make me twitch when I would hear someone talk about going to a megachurch in our city as if it made them a more prestigious Christian. When I would ask how long they had been there, many started attending after the church had grown to its present size, and they had attended to be part of the latest and greatest. That isn't an indictment on those churches or pastors. Those core leaders and pastors burn with a desire to see people come to a personal, saving relationship with Christ and to see their city and world changed, but stepping-stone relationships happen.

Regardless of the stepping-stone, this isn't doing life God's way. Making decisions in relationships out of prayer and love is the goal, not preferences and prominence. When choosing a church, get to know a church's vision and heart. In interpersonal relationships, don't use people for personal needs. Seek for a friendship that is a two-way street. Be content with the spouse you have. Let your hard work and genuine people skills set you apart for advancement at work.

There were so many times it would bother me in pastoral ministry when I would see someone relationally connecting only when they needed something but disappeared after the need was met. Then I realized that there were times I would connect with people to have emotional needs met. When I would back off, it would hurt people. It wasn't the case with the majority of my friendships, but it happened enough that I had to pull the plank out of my own eye when I was so irritated at the stepping-stone behavior of others.

No one is a stepping-stone. Every person is uniquely created by their Heavenly Father, and He has moved heaven and earth through Christ's saving work to provide an opportunity for them to know Him personally and eternally. Each person is infinitely valuable to God, and they should be to us as well. We may not connect with everyone, but we can have the right attitude toward anyone.

So, let's leave the games to the boards, cards, and screens. The ones we play with each other cause too much harm, regret, and damage. Let's love God with all our heart, mind, soul, and strength, and our neighbor as ourselves. Now excuse me as I go get on my helmet to play "Risk" with my wife.

Questions:

1. Which areas from your past impact the way you act and think today? Glory days, regrets over missed opportunities, and/or the reality of past pain?
2. Of the games portrayed in this chapter, which would you have to be careful not to play, or which are you presently playing?
3. Are there any relationships that need to have readjusted boundaries because you are giving someone the focus and attention that should be going to your spouse and/or children?
4. Is there a safe, appropriate person you can discuss this issue with?

Chapter Six

The Bite of Bitterness

. . . looking carefully lest anyone fall short of the grace of God; lest any root of bitterness springing up cause trouble, and by this many become defiled;

—Hebrews 12:15

Repent therefore of this your wickedness, and pray God if perhaps the thought of your heart may be forgiven you. For I see that you are poisoned by bitterness and bound by iniquity."

—Acts 8:22-23

The story of Simon the sorcerer in Acts, chapter 8, is sobering. Prior to his conversion to Christ, he was a man who held sway over the city of Samaria with his demonic power and self-seeking ways. He came to Christ during the miraculous ministry of Phillip who proclaimed the Gospel in word, deed, and miraculous signs in the power of the Holy Spirit. Simon watched the supernatural right before his eyes and was amazed by it all. But, somewhere deep inside, he still wanted the attention and adoration of others. He wanted to be the center of attention while still serving Christ. It is encapsulated in the phrase: "I want God to get the glory, but I want to be the hero."

When any of us tries to be the hero, or the center of attention, it is usually an attempt for others to feed an insatiable need

57

inside of us that is intertwined with something in our past. Trying to re-create the glory days results in wanting others to give us recognition so that we feel like a success as we once saw ourselves. Past pain left unhealed can be like a hungry beast that never gets full. You can push and push through life to achieve, be loved, or be recognized, but when you are given the affirmation you crave, it's never enough. It doesn't live up to the unrealistic expectations you have on yourself, others, and your circumstances and the hunger for something to ease the pain remains. This cycle of brokenness and frustration can often lead to bitterness of the soul. While the Bible doesn't tell us the background of Simon the sorcerer's life, it does tell us that his insatiable and self-serving needs resulted in a man who stated a belief in Christ but wouldn't let Him sit on the throne of his life. Jesus was Savior but hadn't become Lord.

When Peter and some other apostles came to pray for the power of the Holy Spirit upon the new believers of Samaria, Simon was stunned to see what happened. By the laying on of these leaders' hands, new believers received the anointing presence and power of the Holy Spirit. The apostles were living out Jesus' words "freely you have received, freely give." Simon saw something he wanted to take, not receive. His heart issues welled up, and he offered to pay Peter for the Holy Spirit's power, as if it was some magic trick up for sale. Peter confronted Simon, and a part of his rebuke were the two verses from Acts 8 referenced at the beginning of the chapter.

Peter said Simon was poisoned by bitterness and bound by iniquity. That is a scathing indictment. Here was a professing Christian who had received water baptism. But something was wrong. How could this be? Was he insincere in his commitment to Christ? The Scriptures don't tell us this was the case. If he was sincere, how can a follower of Jesus Christ be poisoned by bitterness and bound by iniquity?

To understand this, let me use a visual picture I read in an article. The Old Testament temple was divided into three main sections. The inner most chamber was the Holy of Holies, where the Ark of the Covenant and its ornate covering (Mercy Seat) were kept. Once a year, the High Priest would come in to confess the sins of the nation and sprinkle blood on it to atone (make payment for) the sins of the nation (Leviticus 16). Coming out from the Holy of Holies, one would then enter the Holy Place. In this room was the Altar of Incense, Table of Showbread, and Golden Lampstand. The priests would go in to trim the incense and take care of the candles daily and came in to put new bread on the table once a week. Beyond this room was a larger area called the outer courts where people would bring their sacrifices of worship, repentance, and/or offer praise to God. The priest would offer the sacrifice on their behalf, serving in the role of an intercessor. This process was a foreshadowing of the ministry of Jesus Christ, who became our High Priest and Intercessor when He purchased our freedom through His Blood on the Cross. He is our Intercessor before the courts of heaven, advocating on our behalf (1 John 2:1-2).

As a result of Christ's work, 1 Corinthians 6:19-20 describes us as the temple (dwelling place) of the Lord if we have received the gift of life through Jesus Christ. It says, "Or do you not know that your body is the temple of the Holy Spirit *who is* in you, whom you have from God, and you are not your own? For you were bought at a price; therefore glorify God in your body and in your spirit, which are God's." So with all this in mind, let's take a look at our temple according the template laid out for us in the Scriptures.

Think of your spirit as the Holy of Holies. It is the place the Holy Spirit comes in to reside with you and in you when you become a Christian. The Holy Place is the soul, which is your mind, will, and emotions. The outer courts area is your physical body. When you become a Christian, the Spirit of Christ (Holy Spirit) comes to reside with your spirit. The ongoing journey of deeper growth and surrender is letting God putting His identity, authority, and power on your soul (mind, will, and emotions), which then influences and directs how you use your outer courts (body).

The issue of Simon, the former sorcerer, had nothing to do with there being something lacking in the saving power of Christ. The Holy of Holies can belong to Christ, but the person has yet to give over complete control and authority of the soul and body to Him. Thus, Simon was poisoned by bitterness and bound by sin iniquity in the realms of his temple that he was clinging onto, and Peter confronted him on this.

For far too many of us, we are trying to win the spiritual battle with the best we have to offer, which is our limited, self-seeking, sinful flesh. Thus, there are Christians whose salvation is intact because of the grace of God through Christ, but the Holy Place (mind, will, emotions) and Outer Courts (use of the physical body) are a mess. God's call is for us to let Him transform the whole temple through the indwelling presence of the Holy Spirit in our lives and His power coming upon our lives. 1 Thessalonians 5:23-24 says it this way, "Now may the God of peace Himself sanctify you completely; and may your whole spirit, soul, and body be preserved blameless at the coming of our Lord Jesus Christ. He who calls you is faithful, who also will do it." To sanctify is to set apart and to purify. God promises to do this. When we fight against this sanctifying work of the Holy Spirit, we remain poisoned and bound by the flesh and its desire to be in control. Fewer things are more miserable than a Christian who is poisoned and bound but doesn't know it. They might be unwilling to see it or know it but try instead to put on a good show like all is good. Delusion and deception sure don't help our testimony.

I speak as one who loved the Lord, was called to ministry, served God for years, and strived to be the best husband and father I could. I gave what I thought was my best effort. Yet, there were unresolved issues and sin struggles that I wrestled with for years in my own strength. This inner war took place in my holy place (soul), and ultimately stormed its way into my outer courts (physical life). The sin and its domino effect deeply hurt my wife and kids, as well as impacting hundreds of people.

God, in His mercy and faithfulness, did a transforming work in my life by filling me with a deeper anointing of His Holy Spirit in October of 2015. As John Bevere describes in his book, *The Holy Spirit- An Introduction*, I already had the Holy Spirit positioned in my life through salvation, but I needed the Holy Spirit upon my life to empower and overflow me more than I had previously known. The holy place and outer courts were miraculously overwhelmed by His power and presence, and He witnessed it to me like He did in the book of Acts. Although I felt unworthy of this, it was a gift of grace, just as my salvation was. It was awesome, and it changed my life.

For a number of months, I thought I could run from my past, while living in the new power in the Holy Spirit. Although the power and purity of the new life in Him was real, the human impact of my past couldn't be ignored. The secret I was keeping from my wife was a barrier that had to be removed. When another person decided to detonate my secret, my past sin and secrecy became projectiles that inflicted horrible wounds. It would have been better and right before God and others had I confessed my past on my own. My attempts at self-protection and escaping the past failed, as they should have.

At this darkest moment, God didn't reject me or cast me aside. He had done a miracle in my life and reminded me who I was in Him. My identity didn't change, but I did have to face accountability for my past. The filling and transforming work of the Holy Spirit remained. He held me strong in His power. He knew my heart and the truth of who I was in Him. He showed me that His Spirit would sustain and strengthen me in the difficult days to follow. He also taught me that the deeper work of His Spirit wasn't to be used as a defensive response toward others when I wasn't trusted by them because my past was now their present. Trust would have to be regained over time with people. The deepening relationship with the Holy Spirit was my lifeblood and anchored me as the journey with others continued.

Ultimately, I had to step back from ministry in June of 2016 as part of this accountability. There needed to be an intentional time for healing with my wife and kids, as well as releasing the local church into the Lord's hands for someone else to be their pastor. As I walked through this journey with the oversight of skilled helpers, it became crystal clear that a key root that influenced my past was the sin of bitterness. Over the years, it was a poison that had seeped in and clouded my perspective.

I had to admit I had been bitter toward Barb, believing she saw me as a duty and didn't appreciate me. Although this wasn't the case, bitterness had clouded my perspective. I had bought the false lie that I could make people happy with me and get their approval through performance. I would keep trying to pacify the discontented folks at church and took for granted the positive ones I should have appreciated. I was a peacekeeper, not a peacemaker. A peacekeeper, in a military setting, keeps warring parties apart. The problem isn't permanently resolved, but a temporary ceasefire is maintained. A peacemaker, on the other hand, deals with the core issues of the conflict so that an abiding peace can be achieved.

Keeping people who were in conflict at bay was a lot of work. Most times, long-term resolution wasn't attained. Why do it? I thought it made me a good pastor. What I didn't understand until later was that I became the "fixer" who sought to be approved by both sides until another "flareup" happened. This isn't to smear churches or Christians. I love both, and I believe in the church as one of God's great creations. Christians don't always do church how

61

God wants, but His creation is a great one. My expression of church was as the "fixer," and it was horribly flawed at best and damaging at worst. This idea of being the "fixer" without God's deep solutions is a problem many people, homes, and churches face, but there is a better way.

A peacemaker does the necessary work of dealing with the problems people cause and is committed to finding the root of the problem. Even though it involves hard conversations and, at times, confrontation, the goal is true resolution and, when possible, reconciliation. Jesus was the perfect peacemaker, confronting sin by paying the price for it, and then calling you and me to come to Him through the confession of sin and receiving forgiveness for the sin that separates us from Him. He is always loving, but never enabling. His Word and His Life shine His light of Truth on the corrupted, sinful places in our lives and leave us with no one else to point the finger at. Each of us is to blame for our own sin. Then, He provides His grace for us to experience forgiveness, love, and salvation as we surrender ourselves to Him as our Savior and Lord. Life was always meant to be lived under His leadership. He is the Great Peacemaker.

I didn't learn or apply this truth consistently soon enough, and it resulted in difficult changes personally and professionally. When I rejected peacekeeping for peacemaking, it wasn't popular with those I had enabled. Because I had acted out in secret sin while in the place of the bitter peacekeeper, I ultimately handed my detractors and critics an excuse to reject my attempts to be a peacemaker. The ripple effect of bitterness was a hard pill to swallow.

In the months prior to my resignation, though, I was given a taste of what spiritual leadership could be when done God's way. He finally had me in a place where I was moving in His power and purity as never before. We were seeing miracles happen, people getting saved, bodies being healed, and the oppressive spirit of the enemy being lifted from the church, but the domino effect of past bitterness prevented me from being able to see it through to its conclusion. I am deeply sorry to all those who were hurt by my past sin of bitterness and the other sins that sprouted from it. By God's grace, I can gratefully say it is different now. Extracting the root of bitterness was painful, but it was necessary.

Thankfully though, that wasn't the end of the story. God is greater than my past, and He has forgiven me, restored my marriage and family, and He restored ministry as well. Everything is His and I am very optimistic about the ministry Barb and I share and will share together in Him and the powerful impact He will make through it. He is an awesome God and I praise Him for His grace, mercy, and love. His Spirit poured it out on me, and He wants to pour it out on you. I celebrate His power and presence and want it for you. God wants it for you even more than you do. Wouldn't it be great if you didn't have to crash so hard to learn this lesson?

You don't have to trigger the destructive landmines I triggered. God warned me, as did my wife and others, but I was too self-reliant and secretive. Bitterness is a destructive, sinful deception. It is a poison, but God can give victory over it. He promised Jeremiah, "If you will separate the precious from the vile, you will be as my mouth." This promise is also for you and me. Let's take a few moments and reveal some of the layers of bitterness. It can be painful to peel back the infectious mess, but God wants you to truly be healed and delivered. So, let's rip off the scab and let the infectious, stinky mess out, so that the healing from the core can happen. If you are wondering what this can look like, hopefully the following story will paint a picture of it.

When I met with our marriage counselor for my portion of the one-on-ones, I was focused on the affair that broke the covenant made with God and Barb, and then impacted my children, other family, friends, and others. The counselor gave me homework in which I was to look at my entire life in five-year increments. Under each of these five-year headings, I was to list every painful experience that came to my memory. When I returned for my next section, he had me rank each memory on a pain scale of 1 to 10, as to the level of pain I felt presently about each memory/event listed. Once that was done, he asked me to look through the entire list and rank the top three events/memories in regard to "present tense" pain.

The #1 pain was the day Barb called me home to tell me she had been told of the affair by someone else. She had received an email. As I walked up the driveway, I saw her sitting in our garage, where she had been doing some late spring cleaning. She was sitting on a chair and handed me her phone to read the email. After I read a few lines, I knew what it was, and then I looked into her eyes and saw devastating hurt and betrayal. There are no words to describe the pain of seeing my best friend and wife of twenty-seven years crushed by my inexcusable selfishness and abhorrent behavior.

63

As I recounted the moment in vivid detail to the counselor, he surprised me by following up with this question: "Do you feel the pain inside of you that you felt at that moment?" I nodded yes. "When was the first time in your life you felt the pain you are feeling right now?" I looked at him quizzically. He clarified, "This pain is connected to this moment, but there is a good chance you knew this pain by another name, which is connected to an earlier moment in your life. When was this?" It was stunning how quickly it came to mind. I was seven years old and it was connected to a painful experience in my upbringing. Two events, separated by forty years, had one thing in common: the nature of the pain.

This isn't me blaming anyone else for the sin I committed against my wife. It wasn't a moment of finger pointing. It was a moment of the Holy Spirit giving me a revelation I needed to experience deeper healing and spiritual wisdom. It was the tip of the root of bitterness in my life. The root ran throughout the history of my life, reinforced at different moments by events, people, and even myself, but there was a connection between the two. The Holy Spirit partnered with the counselor to walk me through a process that pulled the root out from the core. Bitterness no longer had a constricting hold on my life.

Previously, I had treated bitterness like I did when I was given the chore of weeding the flower garden in my youth. I would pop the dandelions off just below the surface of the soil so that all you could see were pretty flowers and dark brown mulch. It looked like a job well done on the surface, but the roots were still there. All they needed was periodic rain and some humid summer days to cause the roots to burst forth above the soil once again. Until the root was dug out, the same weed would resurface again and again.

When the heat and rain of life would reveal my dandelions of bitterness, I would tend to focus on the surface issue, repent of it, and snip it off. God was always faithful to forgive, but I was too quick to wipe my hands and consider the job finished. Because the root wasn't removed, the weed would return at some point in the future. Finally, after many years, I had now surrendered to the work of the Holy Spirit, and He used a faithful servant to dig out the root.

God doesn't want you to keep snipping off the outward evidence of bitterness and stopping there. Sure, the dandelion weed on the surface needs to go, but God wants to root out the whole thing. He knows where the bottom of the root is, even if goes deep into places we have inwardly promised ourselves we would never go again. Avoidance and denial don't mean the core issue isn't impacting life on the surface. So, let's briefly look at how bitterness can be rooted in our lives. God's desire and design for you is to be free from bitterness, regardless of its variety.

Bitterness Over the Past

There is bitterness over the brokenness of past relationships. Sometimes it was their fault. At other moments, it was ours, and many times it was a combination of both. When possible, we are to seek healing. Near the end of Romans 12, it tells us "as much as it lies within you, live at peace with all people." "As much as it lies within you" is a vital phrase. It reminds us that no one is responsible for the choices of both people in a relationship. There are moments a person needs to release the relationship into God's hands and stop taking ownership for someone else's decisions.

Other times isn't about letting go, but rather taking responsibility for the decisions we have made. Although you can't control someone's response, it is right to go and ask forgiveness of someone else when you can. The key is to be open to the healing God wants to bring and allow Him to take away the root of bitterness, whether ours or providing an opportunity for someone to experience freedom through our genuine remorse and repentance. You are not responsible for the outcome of your apology, but you can be part of providing an opportunity.

We may have impacted so many, we don't know where to start. Like the tax collector Zacchaeus, we repent and lay our whole lives at Jesus' feet. Jesus celebrates that heart, and He will guide us on this road. Life isn't a never-ending apology tour, but we keep an ongoing openness to asking others for forgiveness when the opportunity presents itself. God moves you from shame to regret. You no longer have to feel like your sin in the end of your story, but you can regret that others' lives were impacted by it.

A second category is the *sins of others*. This refers to the broken relationships or inflicted pain that come from outside of yourself. Bitterness is the common response of a broken heart, and it isn't a healthy choice. Forgiveness is the necessary response of the broken heart, albeit not the one we naturally choose. As I heard Jimmy Evans say in a sermon, "Forgiveness doesn't make them right. It makes you free."

No one's sin against you should be greater than God in your life. You are the one who suffers when you won't forgive. Also, if you have been forgiven by God, then giving forgiveness is the obedient response. Then there is the truth that my sin is no less sinful than anyone else's. As humbling as this is to admit, it underscores a wonderful truth in Christ. His life payment on the cross is the full payment for all sin. This is a life-giving reminder that the blood payment of His perfect, sinless life is enough to pay for the sins committed against us as well. This means those sins don't have to hold us captive. We can be free through forgiveness.

Our pastor, Dr. Tim Bagwell, preached on how Christ took the bite of human sin from the serpent, Satan, and from it, the antibodies of forgiveness through His blood take place. Isn't it amazing that the antibodies for a snakebite come from turning the poison into the cure? The same can be true in our lives. In the Scriptures, Joseph spoke to this in Genesis 50:20, "You meant evil against me, *but* God meant it for good, . . . to save many people alive." His brothers had betrayed him, hated him, sold him as a slave, lied about his death, and left him to a life of loss and servitude. Joseph acknowledged their evil, but then showed how God used it to put Joseph in a place where he could save many, including his family, which would become the nation of Israel. Joseph had the authority and power to take revenge and kill his brothers, but he saw his past pain through God's eyes and allowed God to turn it. God cured Joseph and then made him part of the cure for providing salvation from the famine. God can take your deepest hurts and turn the bite of the enemy into the antibodies of healing through Christ. You are cured to become a cure to help others. This isn't denying the evil of others. It acknowledges it with great clarity, but then decides that God can turn the poison of the sin committed against you into a cure through the power of Christ and His Spirit in you. Pastor Bagwell preached two messages on this on March 4th and 11th, 2018 at Word of Life Christian Center in Lone Tree, Colorado. It is worth your time to order them and learn more how God wants to do this work in your life.

Another type of bitterness is grounded in reflecting and

66

reminiscing over past losses. Grief can embitter us to the core if we let it. God wants to give us freedom. We may always miss someone who has died, but God never intended for bitterness to be the final stop on the journey of grief. While you shouldn't try to avoid the stages and journey of grief, it is important to understand that God wants to lead you through it; He doesn't want you to get stuck in it. Many will describe their ongoing journey of grief. Memories remain and missing someone exists. There is a difference between the one who is paralyzed by bitterness in their grief versus the person who is able to experience the faithfulness of God in the midst of suffering and grief. This is a sensitive area to address because some see the call to move toward healing as requiring them to forget or dishonor the memory of their loved one. Nothing is further from the truth, but the clouds of bitterness make it hard to have a healthy view of grieving. I can't give anyone a timeline for their grief, but God can give someone a destination in it. God can break through this fog, but we must obey Him in spite of the pull of grief that would keep us stuck in a way God never intended.

Finally, broken dreams are a contributing factor in bitterness. The "would-of's, should-of's, could-of's" can erode confidence, fill us with regret, or grip us with anger. Broken dreams cause many to question who they are and where they belong. They are part of that "missed opportunity" that many need redemption from. God wants to give us a secure identity in Christ as an answer to the nagging accusations of "what if." To those who feel deeply disappointed by how their life has gone, the answer of an identity in Christ might sound like a "churchy" answer, but I promise it isn't. It is hard to let go of a dream unfulfilled or a life you had that no longer exists. Bitterness produces a wall of protection that can feel safe, but it ends up building a prison that keeps us from intimacy with God and others.

Knowing and growing in what it means to belong to the Lord transcends the heartbreaking letdowns we experience. Growing in our security in Him is meant to teach us and transform us, but letting go of the past is a hard but necessary step in the process. Most of my vocational dreams have not taken place at this point in my life. In fact, I haven't fulfilled most of the daydreams of my youth. My life isn't done, and those dreams can still come to pass, but they haven't to this point. When I faced my disappointment and came to God with it, I experienced and came to know God's grace. It is ironic that I never felt God's love like I did after my world crashed down into a heap at my feet. He wasn't giving approval of my failures, but He was letting me know His love for me wasn't based in my performance. He secured me in Him, and it brought a deeper healing than I had ever known. He rooted out the deep bitterness I had in my soul. He showed me hope when I felt like an abject failure. Now, I have an authentic hope for the future. Thank God for His ability to overcome bitterness of the past. It sets us free from our self-constructed prisons.

Bitterness in the Present

Some people's bitterness is an all-consuming loneliness. It is an "in-the-moment" feeling. In this place, nobody understands how we feel, think, or view the world. It is as if no one really knows who we are, not even those closest to us. Not being known can be crushing. Either we feel like misfits or believe that others just don't care to know us, or both. It can even lead to wondering if God understands us. If He can understand us, we wonder why He would want to know when we believe no one else does. This is a deep hole to look up from the bottom. It is an orphan spirit that is unable or unwilling to see that the Father makes people His sons and daughters through the work of Christ and indwelling presence of the Holy Spirit.

I am grateful God gave us the Psalms as a key place in Scripture we can turn to when we are at our darkest moments. One of David's songs declares in Psalm 139:1, "O LORD, You have searched me and known *me*." God is the God who knows. He knows you. Does it sound too simple to be true? Well, hear me out before you dismiss it. Whenever we expect another person to truly understand and know us completely, he or she will let us down because the only one who truly knows you is the One who made you. Loneliness and bitterness can come from unmet expectations. God did make us for relationships with others, but we have to understand their place. He made them to fulfill their role, not His. We have to stop expecting others to do what only God can do. People can give us their best and we can give our best to them. That is enough when God has His rightful place in our lives. When this doesn't happen, feelings of rejection seem to rear its ugly head.

When we are overlooked, it communicates that people are scanning for someone more valuable, likable, influential, and desirable. God is the One who sees *(El Roi)*. This is what Hagar said of God when He met her at a time of desperate need when she felt abandoned and hopeless. Paul said in Romans 5:8 that when we were yet sinners, Christ died for us. He sees us when we don't want to be seen. He sees us at our worst and offers us His best. This can remove the bitterness of being overlooked and replace it with the gratitude of being seen by Him.

For some it may not be someone overlooking them, bur overworking them that leads to bitterness. An overworked person can feel like that rented mule that is being beat and used until there is nothing left. Some feel no more valuable than the paycheck they bring home, the tasks they do, and the demands they meet. Out of bitterness, we stop asking for help and just trudge through, getting more bitter by the month, by the year. Jesus says, "Come to me all you are heavy burdened and I will give you rest." He says that "His yoke is easy and His burden is light." He told Martha that "she worried about many things." When Peter was focused on God's plan for John, Jesus said, "What is that to you? You follow me." He invites us to freedom when He teaches, "whatever you do, do it all for the glory of God." When you are overworked, He wants to lighten your burden so that you aren't bitter. Give your best for Him; but don't let the demands of others or the self-imposed demands of co-dependency keep you from intimacy with God.

When you have unmet hopes in any present circumstance, He wants to be the Hope you have by faith. As I wrote these words, the Dave Crowder song "Lift Your Head Weary Sinners" played on Spotify. This song is a great encouragement to me. When the church we attend, Word of Life Christian Center, does their rendition of this song, it lifts my spirit and often brings me to tears. I am overwhelmed at His grace and love over my life. I am known and seen by our burden-lifting God who gives hope and faith. Bitterness melts away, and I wonder why I held onto it as long as I did.

Bitterness Over One's Future Prospects

There can be hopelessness about how we think our

circumstances will turn out. There can be cynicism about people, along with their motives and agendas. There can be brokenness in our view of God, resulting in lies about Him seeming to be true. God responds to our hopelessness by saying in Romans 5 that "hope does not disappoint us because God has poured out His love in our hearts." He observes our cynicism about people and He points us to grace. He gives us grace and calls us to give it to others. We tend to judge people by their actions, but we want others to judge based on our intentions. Grace allows us to see what God sees and give people forgiveness when there seems to be little motivation to do so. When our view of Him is broken, He gives us the Truth of His Word and His Holy Spirit to guide us into Truth. Looking at the future with a broken view of God tends to push us toward alternatives apart from God and His Truth. When we seek counsel about the future from those who don't see God in their future, adding their brokenness to our brokenness doesn't add up to the sum of clarity and clear thinking and doing.

***

His Truth, through His Word and His Spirit, will pierce through the fog of aimlessness and the despair of hopelessness. It is never His will for you to be poisoned by bitterness and bound by sin. His call is to everyone and for everyone. Take it from me, or better yet, receive it from Him. He wants to take bitterness from you. Having your past redeemed, whatever your story is, has a lot to do with letting Him root out the bitterness and then deepening your roots in Him. There is a lot in this chapter to think about, and I hope you give yourself the time and space with God and yourself, and even others to do so. It is worth the time and so are you.

Chapter Seven

Rationalized Compromise

Recently, I heard a pastor say something like this, "We like what the Bible says about others. We just don't like what it says about us." The message was talking about marriage, and I chuckled inwardly about the truth of this tendency. Throughout our marriage, I wanted Barb to do what the Bible said in regard to her being my wife. But, somehow, I gave less scrutiny, usually when I was being critical of her, to what the Bible told me as a husband. As I have spent more time focusing on what God's Word says to me as a husband, it is amazing how it left room for God to speak to my wife about what matters to Him in her life. The irony though, is that she looks better and better as I let God work on me. Could it have been that by spending too much time thinking about how she could be better, I was blinded to areas of weakness and sin in my life? Hmm.

When our past needs redeeming, we can try to fix the people around us, while missing the need for some real-life work on ourselves. It goes something like this. "If I can just order my life, relationships, and career, then I can make up for what I didn't have before." Some try to recreate the glory days by putting pressure on others to help fulfill their past dreams. Maybe you have seen the parent driving their child in an unhealthy way as the parent recounts what they did in their day or could have been in their day? Others feel they missed it and push others to achieve where they felt they failed. The ones in pain can overcompensate from one extreme to the other. Some perpetuate their past pain and abuse on the next

71

generation, while others run from it so hard, they enable the next generation by being too lenient.

Regardless of the expression, the common thread in these examples is other people become the tools used to deal with our past. True, selfless love, as God expresses it through us, wants His best for someone else, not our best for them. Sometimes, the two plans are aligned, but other times they are not. We can rationalize a withering critique of others, while missing that others pay the price from our lack of self-awareness or dealing with our past. Just as my marriage did better when I let God's Word speak to me and stop trying to be the Holy Spirit's helper for my wife, so can each of us be more effective when we start with what God is saying to us. This isn't meant to imply parents stop guiding children or taking an "I don't care" attitude. Rather, I am saying that our credibility is more consistent as we walk with people, not drive them blindly while running or reacting to the past.

This principle rings true in other areas of life as well. It doesn't take much to see how the world as a whole, and individuals in particular, could be fixed if they would just listen to God's Word. Although it is true that every person is a work in progress, there is a credibility gap if we let the Bible read others but not ourselves as well. Simply put, I can accurately point out the problems of others, but miss the glaring weakness that others see in me. When this selective reading of the Bible happens, it is a contradiction that hinders a Christian's witness. Instead of seeing God's Word as the Truth that speaks to all people, personal contradiction can influence others to see the Bible as a selective sword to be pulled out when it applies to others. The Bible is a two-edged sword that needs to be applied to the "man in the mirror," as well everyone else. So, as we decide on how we use the Word of God, we have choices. Let's look at some of them.

If one chooses to reject what the Bible says because of a flawed messenger, then he/she misses its transforming power. In addition, one risks making sweeping, rejecting generalizations about the Bible and/or Christians, often not based in truth or accurate knowledge. Another option is to edit the Bible to fit our time, so that it is less offensive in the areas we have different opinions. In this way of thinking, we are making a supposedly archaic book speak to contemporary times. The problem with this is that people rewrite or edit out timeless, eternal truths as if they were cultural messages for one time and not ours. The editor treats truths about ethics, sexuality, and behavior as if they were "sifting" out Old Testament dress codes. We keep the truth that God is love, but lose the truth that God is Holy and that we are answerable to Him on how we live our lives.

Some choose a method of interpretation in which they accurately see the sin in the world or the sin of a specific person but miss the shortcomings and sin in their own lives. Granted, we can't wait to speak God's truth until we have mastered it perfectly. If that was the standard, then God's Word wouldn't be spoken at all because all have sinned. But it is vital that we speak His Truth from a place that recognizes that we are all a work in progress. We must humbly admit where He is working on us while we are also challenging others. Those who ignore the essence of self-awareness are blind to how God's Word needs to read them. As a result, there are too many experts on how the Bible is indicting others. In this case, a person could be one hundred percent correct on the sin being confronted in another but keep smacking people with the plank in their own eye. They are technically right, but fewer and fewer are willing to listen to a blind guide.

A final example of an unhealthy response is to become so transfixed with one's failure in the sight of God that the reality of sin doesn't lead to the gift of grace. Self-condemnation misses the restoration of forgiveness and the promise of a new identity in Christ. The danger of this mindset is that we don't see past our failures to embrace a full life in Christ. This person doesn't condemn the world but instead disqualifies themselves. In his book, *The Father's Embrace*, Jack Frost talked about how he spent years of his life trying to perform his way in order to gain the approval of God and others. Chasing the ghosts of his past pain and regret, he wore everyone out in his life, including himself. When he finally experienced the love of the Heavenly Father, it changed everything. Although one can't skip the step of seeing the truth of sin personally, the truth of grace must also be experienced. There are people who don't do this. They believe they are the exception to God's grace in order to flog themselves with ongoing punishment for their sin instead of resting in the finished work of Jesus Christ.

After all these examples, one may wonder where the hope is in the midst of these battles. My description could lead one to conclude that most people have a rationalizing compromise in some area of life. I do believe that is true, but there is a confident hope in the relentless love of God. He isn't willing to leave us in this state of disarray. He wants so much more for you. He has provided the pathway to MORE through the redeeming work of His Son, the empowering work of His Holy Spirit, and the revelatory work of His Scripture, and for you to live in the fullness of His MORE, rationalized compromise must be defeated and dismantled. God wants it, and I believe you want it as well. So, let's dig in on some ways rationalized compromised can be defeated and destroyed in your life. *Redeeming Our Past* comes when His Truth dismantles the structures we built in our lives that won't stand the test of time. He builds something in us and through that will ripple through eternity. As Jesus promised in John 8:32, "And you shall know the Truth and the Truth shall make you free." Here are some areas that must be defeated so we can experience the victory God has for us.

Defeating the Rationalized Compromise of . . .

The Flawed Messenger

It starts with misdirected discernment. You see, many are correct when they point out the contradictions in a flawed messenger. The hypocrisy of inconsistency in the messenger is glaring and stand out to the discerning person, but therein lies the problem that can lead to rationalized compromise. The person who rejects the truth because of the messenger has misunderstood why they have the gift of discernment. Discernment is the ability to recognize what is spiritually true from what is spiritually false. It is the ability to see past the surface and understand what is really going on in people, groups, and circumstances. A discerning person can spot a phony and see ulterior motives, but tragically, many use this amazing ability to condemn, reject, and marginalize people as well as groups.

The gift of discernment was meant to be used to know how to speak truth and confront lies, but the gift isn't just for that purpose. It also gives insight on how to pray for someone because you know what is really going on at the core. Discernment was meant to give wisdom to know how to build relational bridges because you can see the deep need and real hurt of another person. It was meant to lovingly present needed solutions to deep problems because the discerner sees the real issue at hand. It is meant to provide

74

opportunities for reconciliation not condemnation.

If you have discernment, please understand this gift was never meant to be your tool for the rationalized compromise of rejecting the message of God because of the failures of the messengers of God. It is a mistake to think everyone around you sees the blind spots you see. Yes, there are dangerous, devious people that need to be exposed, but many others struggle with their sin and blindness to cover up insecurities, hurt, and fears. You could be an instrument of healing in God's hands, but if you use your discernment for the rationalized compromise of harsh condemnation, you become the thing you despise - an unjust person. When you decide to respond to someone's hypocrisy with a condemning response, you are now your own version of a flawed messenger. This rationalized compromise in your life can cause the truths you see to be rejected by others because they see a bitterness in you. Discernment was meant to break the cycle of brokenness, not keep it going.

Discerning people have an opportunity to be an exhorter. An exhorter has the ability to see God's Truth for a person or situation and then speak to the person with authority, while still being lifegiving. The goal of the exhorter is for God to be magnified and His Truth to be known. It is for Him to be worshipped, submitted to, and lived for in our world. It isn't for bitterness, self-righteousness, or isolation. Confronting a flawed messenger is only effective if you are a faithful messenger yourself. Let go of the rationalized compromised of misused discernment, and you will be able to recognize and confront the shortcomings of a particular messenger without dismissing the eternal message.

Editing the Bible

There is a humanistic way of thinking that has so saturated our culture that we often don't recognize its impact on us. It is based on the belief that we are the result of evolutionary development instead of unique people who are made in God's image. As a result, humanistic thinking concludes that people are more intelligent today than at any time previously because we are continuing our progress toward our full evolutionary potential. Advances in technology, medicine, space travel, scientific discovery, and education are used as evidence of this. Thus, the Bible is viewed as an outdated, archaic book that needs to be left in the sands of time, in lieu of the views of progressive enlightenment of the best and brightest. Those who hold to Scripture as God's truth are viewed as threats to progress who need to be cast aside as intellectual Neanderthals. They are not the fittest and their survival should be based on whether or not they embrace the superior truths of human advancement.

When this thought enters the church, then unpopular teachings on sin, morality, sexuality, and human relationships are revised or edited out completely. It leads to large sections of the church holding to eternal truths about love and grace but discarding moral accountability before God. In this humanistic approach to Scripture, man isn't made in God's image as much as God is being made into the image man wants "him" to be. Humanity is with a capital "H," while God is reduced to a lower case "g." If you have this struggle, your challenge is embracing humility as a key pathway to change.

Why is this a challenge? Because those who edit or dismiss the Bible as inferior or outdated don't tend to be humble in their handling of the Bible. They view those who don't agree with them as intellectually inferior. If others just listened to you and became smarter, they would come to your conclusions. In other words, disagreeing with you has more to do with your intelligence and others' ignorance. In fact, some might even dismiss my words with this type of accusation. God invites all of us to humility, because compared to Him, we all have much to learn.

God's Word calls each of us to the foundational conclusion that God is God and we are not. He made our world and each of us. We (including me) are accountable to Him for what we do with Him, His Truth, and the life He has given to each of us. So, if the rationalized compromise of editing the Bible is to be set aside, a person must be willing to see and accept three fallacies.

First, humanistic arrogance is based in self-diagnosed truth. When a person decides his or her own doctrines of sin and truth, then God is no more than the construct of their own intellect, feeling, and instincts. In other words, their god is no bigger than them. In their mind, He becomes the product of creation, rather than the Creator. Once a person reduces who God is, there often is a domino effect on how they view other people as well. It can affect the way we treat those we see as ignorant or inconvenient. This can be seen in how many view and treat the old and young around us.

Instead of honoring the oldest among us, we risk viewing them as outdated, clueless, and burdensome. Instead of viewing us as standing on their shoulders, we view them as being a drain on our resources and a hurdle to the future.

When it comes to human beings inside the womb, the intellectual elites ignore the very science they proclaim to live by and dehumanize the baby inside a woman. It is indisputable that a child in the womb is a distinct being from the mother. Ultrasound technology shows a developing person inside the womb, but we ignore it willfully under the guise of humanistic advancement and personal choice. Thus, abortion is seen as a women's rights issue instead of a human rights issue. Rational thought is traded for baseless conclusions. Because the child is weak, unseen, and unheard, it is subservient to the wishes of the strong, male and female. Millions of children are killed every year around the world. It is largely the result of the humanistic arrogance of self-defined truth. If humanistic arrogance is rejected though, people can embrace the fullness of being made in God's image without disregarding, discarding, and oppressing the weaker among them.

A second key fallacy that leads to editing or rejecting God's Truth is confusing innovation with insight. There isn't an automatic correlation between an advancement in technology and moral and spiritual insight. Knowledge doesn't always lead to wisdom. Every advance stands on the shoulders of the work of others who came before us. As each generation stands on the shoulders of the innovation of others, they have the opportunity to build on it, expand it, and learn more of the creative potential of the world God made. Sometimes, innovation has been used to make the lives of humanity better. Other times, it has been used to increase suffering and destruction. Many innovations are amoral and are neither good nor evil. It depends on the motive and intent of the user on whether it becomes moral or immoral.

Look at social media as an example. Social media and the many other expressions of the internet has been used to connect people globally. Dictatorships have been toppled by its ability to be used as a tool to overcome suppressive regimes that restrict freedom of the press. But, at the same time, this same technology platform is being used for exponential evil. Pornography and human sex trafficking are at pandemic levels. Millions of girls, boys, women, and men are ravaged and sold, and some are even killed in the pursuit of sexual addiction. Hundreds of millions of others are enslaved to sexual addiction through various forms of pornography. Pornography is crippling the ability of people to be intimate in healthy ways in marriage.

Innovation in society doesn't always lead to insight of the soul. This isn't a call to returning to a less-advanced society. It is a call to understand that just because we have conveniences that make life better on the outside, this doesn't necessarily lead to people becoming better on the inside. Every person has a body, a soul (mind, will, and emotion), and a spirit. The Father gave us His Word, His Son, and His Holy Spirit so that we could be in a personal relationship with Him. This allows our loving Father to take His rightful place in our lives by the authority of Jesus Christ, through the power and presence of the Holy Spirit. The insights and inspiration that comes from this relationship does away with our rationalized compromises. We are the better for it.

Selective Confrontations

The essence of this rationalized compromise starts with the right belief that God's Word is the ultimate source of truth for our world collectively and each person individually. The problem comes if one chooses to build the wrong structure on this right foundation. In this example, rationalized compromise selects the truths that apply to others, while ignoring or neglecting the ones that apply to us. Thus, although solid Truth is being presented to the world at large, the lack of self-awareness leads to inconsistency that hurts the receptivity of the message and the credibility of the messenger.

I write this in the aftermath of the 2016 presidential election. It was stunning in its display of unhealthy behavior. Many Christians chose to trumpet a political platform that both supported and contradicted the principles of God's Kingdom. On one side, some Christians voted for a candidate who rightly said he would defend the lives of unborn children in how he appointed Supreme Court justices. But this same candidate was objectionable in the way he talked and treated people outside the womb of different races, nationalities, and gender. Too many Christians in this political camp would point out the sins of their political opponent but excuse away or minimize the sins of this candidate.

On the flip side, there were Christians who supported a candidate who spoke of building community and defending the weak or overlooked among us, which was good, but at the same time, this candidate spoke of abortion as being a women's rights issue when innocent human lives are being taken every day against their will. Children in the womb are disregarded in the name of something called choice. Christians supporting this candidate would condemn the bigotry of their political opponent, while condoning the contradiction of their candidate on the value of life. As a result, many Christians found themselves being selective in their confrontations and thus lacking credibility on both sides of the political aisle. I am editing this chapter in April 2018, and the climate hasn't changed. Selective confrontations are happening, with both sides raging against the other, yet unwilling or unable to see the contradictions in their own stances. Hopefully, you aren't one of those slamming this book shut just because I urge you to consider potential inconsistencies in how you confront things.

The Scriptures make it clear in 2 Timothy 2:1-4 that we have a mandate from God to pray for our leaders, regardless of whether we agree with them. Too often I have heard followers of Christ use freedom of speech as a rationalized compromise for hateful, venomous words and attitudes toward political opponents instead of obeying the truth of God in genuine intercession for their leaders. Passionate disagreement is a privilege of free speech, and standing for the Truth of God's Word is a must, but how we do it and how we sound in expressing this freedom matters to God and should matter to us.

Another way the rationalized compromise of selective confrontation needs to be addressed is in the tendency to redefine our sin while laser focusing on others' sin. When I sin, it is a personal choice to do wrong, embrace selfishness and express rebellion against God's authority over my life. It isn't a mistake or accident. But when I am selective, I can redefine my sin to be less sinful or not wrong at all from my point of view. Two red flags are common in this. The first is when a person isn't able to admit when he or she is wrong or chooses not to admit an area of needed growth or healing from a past pain. One could challenge my assertion and say that some people are just private and don't choose to share with the masses. That is fine, but then this person should choose to be just as discreet in being critical of others. In other words, if I choose to be private with whom I share my weaknesses, then I shouldn't be so public about sharing another's shortcomings.

This isn't a call to embracing shame as a way of living. A Christian's identity has been forged and anchored in the forgiving work of Jesus Christ. None of us should live in an ongoing, shame-filled rehearsal of the past. He has declared forgiveness and freedom for all those who call on Him for salvation. Through His saving work, He makes people His sons and daughters. The confidence that comes from this identity is anchored in a humble heart, since it was His goodness that did all of this. A person who is secure in their identity in Christ can admit when they are wrong and ask for forgiveness in the areas they are still a work in progress. This type of life enhances personal credibility because it offers hope, not a false veneer of self-righteousness. Knowing who you are in Christ gives you the security to admit and confess you are wrong without your personal identity being at stake.

Rationalized compromise, on the other hand, presents self-righteousness as a way to protect our image while casting stones at others. A self-righteous person may be accurate about the sin he or she is confronting, but their lack of Spirit-led self-awareness undermines their credibility. A Spirit-led life of gratitude to God results in confidence in His Word and our place in His Family. It empowers us to present His Truth to our world with a gentleness that invites others to see Him. It gives us the courage and resolve to take risks in expressing His love.

Self-Condemnation Apart from Grace

The final example of rationalized compromise in this chapter expresses itself a bit differently from the others, but is dangerous nonetheless. A person in this trap is so focused on the depth of their sin, they doubt the power of God to forgive or restore them. This person's past is chocked full of personal condemnation. It can be from one's own sin, or the personal pain from the impact of others' sin committed against another. Whether it is one or both, it becomes a suffocating fog of self-hatred and hopelessness. A person in this trap sees themselves as the scapegoat, damaged goods, or an object of rejection. In this place, one can become the self-perpetuating victim. Although truly hurt by their past, this person passes on this pain to others. They can do this by pushing others away in self-protection or suffocating others by their personal neediness and self-absorption. Whichever way it manifests, a person trapped in the lie of self-condemnation fails to believe God can heal him or her from the impact of personal sins and/or the sins of others.

This rationalized compromise is based in two key deceptions. The first is not seeing self-loathing as a form of idolatry. Idolatry is when a person puts something or someone in first position in their lives in place of God. The deception is that we usually think of idolatry in terms of elevating a person, pursuit, or possession above God but don't include self-loathing or self-hatred as part of idolatry. I mean, if I think I am beyond forgiveness or inherently damaged goods, how can that be idolatry? Putting anything above God is idolatry. I am no less self-centered if I put my self-pity above God as opposed to arrogance or pride. Either way, one's eyes are not looking at God but rather at self.

A second tragedy from self-condemnation is when a person disqualifies themselves from God's plan rather than discovering their place in it. A prideful person misses God's plan because he or she is obsessed with pursuing their own plan, but a self-condemned person misses God's plan because of being obsessed with believing he or she can't be part of it. The enemy of your soul, the devil, is just as satisfied to keep you on the sideline, as with getting you distracted with your own game plan. Jesus Christ wants you to know your identity in Him and to experience the freedom of His forgiveness.

After spending most of my adult life as a local church pastor, I had to step away for a time because of the consequences of my sin. Even though this time was needed for accountability and consequences, God wasn't just about discipline. He was also about restoring and redeeming. Never in my life did I experience the love and kindness of God more than when I was at my lowest. It was a surprise that changed my life. I had been a Christian for decades but had been driven by my own self-condemnation that I had carried from childhood. I pushed to be the best pastor, best husband, best father, and the best in any pursuit. If I succeeded enough, maybe the inner, aching pain would go away. I pushed people away and had a hard time accepting others' love or acceptance because I didn't believe they meant it, or I didn't believe I deserved it.

His love led to a strange irony. My life was a heap of ashes, yet the foundation of Christ's love and forgiveness remained and shined through the darkest moments. My wife and I walked through the hard road of healing. We went through life-giving Christian counseling and submitted ourselves under the spiritual authority of another pastor and local church. I was accountable to the denominational authority structure who oversaw the ministry restoration plan. Through all of it, God met me in a new way, even in the difficult moments.

I saw most of my friends and peers disappear. It reminded me there are consequences to sin, but as I let go of self-condemnation and experienced the Father's embrace in a way I had never known, the pain miraculously faded away. It is ironic that at a time when what I had was the least impressive from a human perspective, I have never had more contentment and peace. Barb and I have never been more in love than we are right now. I enjoy and love my kids and grandkids like never before. I love the church and am not bitter. God has helped me forgive people I needed to forgive, including myself, and accept forgiveness from Him and others. My calling as a pastor is stronger than ever. What ministry will look like in the future is in God's hands. But life is good and God is great!

***

So, whatever your rationalized compromise, let the light of God's Truth shine on it, reveal it for what it is, and remove it from your life. Humble yourself and come to Him as the hope of your today and the promise of your tomorrow. I share with you what my pastor, Dr. Tim Bagwell reminds us on a regular basis: YOU ARE WHO GOD SAYS YOU ARE!

Chapter Eight

Breaking the Ties That Bind

I was sitting with my friend Jason on the patio of a local burger restaurant. We were eating our mac n cheeseburger, which is, well . . . a mac n cheeseburger - enough said. The shopping center was crowded as we watched cars drive past and people bustling from one place to another. Jason cut through the air with this statement, "Most of these people are slaves." He then explained that most were driving cars and living in houses that engulfed them in debt to the point that they had to be slaves to their work just to keep up with it all. He wryly described a person going to work to pay for the flat-screen television bought on credit to veg in front of each evening. He described this as an enslavement to debt.

We commiserated that this wasn't the way God intended work to be. Yes, we are supposed to give our best for the glory of God, which includes our work, but it was never meant to be an endless cycle of shackles. We were meant to be living out God's will for our lives in spiritual freedom that will incorporate all of life, including finances. Not only that, but His freedom impacts all of life, including time, relationships, work, finances, leisure, church, etc. He wants to empower us to love others with His love and have relationships the way the Bible describes. We are called to be free so we can be available for God to weave His plans into our schedule because we aren't so transfixed on survival alone. Rather than an endless hamster wheel of impossible expectations, God wants us to be free in Him to live life without the crushing enslavement that traps so many.

Some may dismiss this as "pie in the sky" dreaming of two friends who were eating too many gourmet burgers. The burger part might be true, but it also might be true that dismissiveness can be a good cover for defensiveness. If each of us took a deep breath and looked around at our world, we could easily see how many have chosen to live life that isn't as God intended. We could see the ropes that bind us and then focus on learning how God wants to set us free. The amazing hope is that we can know and live out the promise of freedom, the power of freedom, and the practice of freedom.

So, what are some of those ropes that point to any of us having an area of spiritual enslavement, of being trapped in a cycle that needs to be broken? For some, the redemption of the past requires them to be honest about their present way of thinking and living. Past regrets, memories of a glory day gone by, and the infections of past pain can lead to an awful lot of coping mechanisms. It would be quite daunting to try and give a complete list what this looks like. I believe it would be more beneficial to demonstrate categories and examples that can help you and the Lord evaluate where you are. Remember, the goal is your freedom, and the peace that comes from knowing who you are in Him.

To get you thinking, here are some behaviors and thought patterns that can spur your mind. It includes examples I hope sound familiar. You might add others to the list, and we could probably relate to each other quite a bit. But remember, the goal isn't to have a camaraderie in a collective prison but rather see the places that the Spirit of God wants to shatter chains and set you free.

They Can't Do It Without Me, or At Least I hope So

Many of you know the drill. Overcommit in the name of helping others and then get embittered with your life and others as you get overwhelmed. A person in this trap may whine, complain, or explode in fits of anger. In these frustrated places, they tell people "if you want it done right, you have to do it yourself." Although bitter or frustrated over all the work they must do, they still do other people's work for them. Granted, many are willing to let them, but the complainer also put themselves there. When someone acts like this, it is because they want to be needed, to be seen as irreplaceable, or just get too much identity from being the hero. I did this at different times during pastoral ministry. On one hand, I was deeply committed to developing leaders and helping others find their best in Christ. When I stayed focused on that, I was effective. But when

I overtaxed my life with making sure others needed me to solve their problems, I missed the boat and ultimately faced burn out.

Guess what? After eighteen years at the same church, I stepped away. After my resignation, I was unemployed for most of the summer, looking for work. Besides getting much needed rest, I had to watch as the church moved on after I left. They stopped almost all of the unnecessary stuff I did and didn't miss it. God allowed me to see the chain of "they can't do it without me" break free from me and them, even though it was painful to experience at moments. I had come to resent the chain, yet acted as if I needed that chain. When you arrange life in such a way in which you think people can't do it without you, it enslaves all involved in a lie that needs to be exposed in the light of God's Truth.

Finances/Debt

This isn't some diatribe against doing well. It is an assertion that many people are enslaved in their lives when it comes to money. For many, it is based in a lack of contentment. You see it when people's standard of living is whatever they make, even if there are increases of pay over the years. So, instead of money being a tool, it is a trap.

Some live in the trap of survival living and never have enough money to consistently pay the bills. Life is ongoing cycle of financial emergencies. Others have financial overflow but won't let it be enough. The house has to be better, the cars have to be newer, or the technology must be the best. The great paycheck becomes collateral for leveraging debt, rather than a springboard for saving, giving, or paying off debt.

A third group is enslaved with the self-righteous view that they are superior to those around them who have less. It is a condescending mindset that truly believes that if others just did things the way you did, they would have what you have. Successful people do have much to teach others, but those who are grateful for their blessings approach it in a healthier way. Those who don't view blessing through the lens of gratitude toward God can view their money and possessions as something they have earned and have a right to control and protect from others. This way of thinking enslaves the person who has succeeded with a prejudice that sees others as threats, mooches, or inferior to them.

Money can make someone feel more or less valuable depending on where you they on the spectrum. If a person becomes stingy in regard to their money with God and people, they are enslaved. The irony is that none of us get to take it with us after we die. In too many cases, I have seen a person's financial legacy be evaporated by long-term care expenses or by family members who argue over who gets what after the person has died. Being stingy causes a person to miss the opportunity for their financial success to be a legacy for the future generations and a blessing in this present generation for God's Kingdom and others.

This lie can manifest itself through living on credit instead of what you can afford, surviving from one financial crisis to another, or greedily holding onto what is yours while looking down your nose at others. All three represent links in a chain that needs to be broken. God wants you to be free to be content in Him. Free to learn to live on what you make. Free to say no until you can afford to pay for it without incurring debt. Free to give generously and joyfully to the Lord and others, while leaving a legacy for your children and grandchildren. Free to let money be a tool at your disposal, not a trap for your destruction.

Shame

We all have a past. Specifically, I mean we all have actions, words, and attitudes we aren't proud of when we think about them. Our past sin hurt others and ourselves. The ripple effect and reminders of it can plague us. Driven to try to make up for it, we can push harder to do right, but for some, it never seems to be enough. The ghosts of the past nip at our heels. I am describing a person driven by shame. Shame is the enemy of repentance and restoration. There are natural consequences for our sins, and at times, it is severe. That being said, you can accept consequences without believing the past is unforgiveable.

Unfortunately, there can be people who don't want you to move on after a failure. They want you to live in misery. In part, it is to control you, in part to punish you, and in part to evaluate your sincerity. In contrast, God has the amazing ability and capacity to forgive and provides freedom from shame, even when sin's consequences are still in view. God wants to free you from shame because shame keeps your failure from becoming a testimony of God's redeeming power. He wants to move you from shame to healthy regret. Regret for the past recognizes that others were impacted by your sin and you don't want to do that to people again. Repentance and remorse over personal sin is necessary. Unending shame, on the other hand, traps a person in a cycle of unworthiness and self-hatred.

After my failure, I was devastated. For the eight months until it became public, I lived with shame and self-hatred, although I had been forgiven, and God was doing the miraculous in the church. The problem was that my sin was a secret. I was hiding it from others out of the fear of rejection and also using it as a whip to beat myself daily. Once the secret was out, it was horrifying to see my wife and family hurt and embarrassed, as well as the hundreds impacted in the church and community. I did a pretty good job of jumping into the deep end of the pool when it came to shame.

One day my daughter said, "Dad, you need to stop apologizing!" She was mad. Ironically, it wasn't because I had sinned and hurt the family and church. It was because she was concerned I would stay in this place of self-condemnation for good. I had to let God show me I could stand tall in His forgiveness, even while walking through the journey of repairing relationships I had damaged. When the chains of shame were broken, I could then see a bright future even while having to account for my past. I could be submissive under my authorities and contrite for my sin but also not wait for someone else's permission to rise up within and with others after I had fallen down.

Repentance is true sorrow for one's sins before God and others. It is a surrender to Him and an about face away from the self-centered living. It leads a person toward God. Shame moves a person away from God and others. Repentance leads us back to God and others. If you have failed, be repentant before God. Be humble and remorseful with others as well. Be teachable and accountable for the necessary life changes needed to not travel this road again. But also remember that God wants you to experience forgiveness. He wants you to get up in Him and move forward. Consequences aren't always in your control. That is the harsh reality of the choices we make. In the face of that struggle, God's forgiveness and restoring power break the chains and give us His view. The past doesn't have

87

to be our future.

You can't make someone trust you again. But you can be trustworthy. You can't make someone forgive you. But you can live a life as one who has been forgiven. You can't undo what you did. But you can let God do something new in your life. The chain of shame is a heavy burden that can crush you, if you let it. Every sin has a consequence, but it doesn't have to be the end.

Every sin has already been paid for by Jesus Christ through the blood payment of His life on the cross. He isn't pleased with your sin, but He has provided a payment for it. He loves you and wants you to know repentance can lead to restoration, and restoration can lead to renewal. Paul said he was the chief of sinners but that Christ had saved him. The murderous persecutor of Christians was now one who declared the greatness of Christ's forgiveness. The murderer was now a messenger. God sure knows how to set someone free. Pastor Bagwell reminded us that Jesus cures us that we might be part of the cure for others.

Performance/Approval

If I do enough, respond enough, or become enough, I will be loved or affirmed. This is the enslavement of the hamster wheel. Kevin Myers, in his book *Home Run*, talked about the backward way people are taught to seek value themselves, as opposed to God's design, which gives value and purpose. In God's design, He has us start and end with our relationship with Him. He then builds our inner character from this place. From that character, we can become a trustworthy person who can have healthy relationships. And from those relationships of trust, we can do the tasks of our lives with competence and excellence. Myers used the baseball diamond to portray God's design. God is our home plate, where we begin and end. First base is character. Second base is the community of our relationships. Third base is the competence we bring to our tasks. We then finish where we began - with God. He is the home plate on which all of our lives must be grounded.

Our world distorts it and often makes our performance home plate. It turns the bases one notch counterclockwise so that third base is now home plate. Then it has us run the bases backward.

We begin and end with tasks, and then focus on people, then character, and lastly, God. The results leave us wanting.

People spend their lives trying to achieve and later realize they steamrolled or ignored people in the pursuit of their goals. So, after starting with tasks, many will discover that relationships are needed and that success alone doesn't bring peace. But in the pursuit of relationships, we often experience brokenness because our character isn't anchored in such a way that we are trustworthy to the people who know us. So, we turn our attention to the personal development of our character. Ultimately, that leads us to the harsh conclusion that we can't do this on our own strength and that maybe the idea of God we dismissed or ignored for a time wasn't so far-fetched after all.

In fact, after the pursuit of success, relationships, and character apart from Him, we realize we needed Him for all three of these things all along. So, we finally come home to God, where He welcomes us with open, loving arms. This backward pursuit sees God as the final attempt, rather than the place we begin and end. When kids run the bases out of order, it is tee ball. It is amusing to watch in five-year-olds but not so much in adults who use it as a pattern for living.

We can be freed from the chains of performance and approval by running the base paths of life as God intended. It is the freedom that comes from beginning and ending with Him. When we have strikeouts or don't get on base, He teaches us, corrects us, loves us, and He puts us back in the game. He doesn't cut us from the team. This is awesome because there are times we would have rather stayed in the dugout. He has us get back up to bat and try again.

There is great freedom in doing life His way. Start and end with Him. Let Him use His Truth to shape our character. From that, He will make you trustworthy so that people can feel safe in relationship with you. As you build from there, then the training you receive to be good at what you do can be effective. You seek to be competent and give your best at whatever you do. By being teachable and continuing to train, your excellence is added to your relationships, character, and relationship with God. It all targets you for home plate where you and God can celebrate the scores in your life. This cycle can continue for the glory of God and all He has planned for you. Sure beats running the bases the wrong way and wondering why you never score.

Addiction

Simply put, when we cope with unhealthy substances and behaviors, we believe we can't make it without them in our lives. We are enslaved to it, and it becomes an addiction. For me, it was food. I would get stressed, and cope with a late-night bag of chips or something fried. Others use alcohol. It could be drugs, whatever their source or legal status. Some find solace in pornography or other expressions of sexuality outside of God's design and plan. The list goes on and on. Social media, video games, cutting, gambling, gossip, workaholism, and more are on this destructive list.

But there is freedom in the power of the Holy Spirit, the truth of God's Word, and in a saving relationship with Jesus Christ. In some cases, God heals instantaneously, removing the draw and desire of the addictive behavior in an instant. For others, the journey to freedom involves a process where we travel with God and others. It can involve counseling, recovery, and medical care for a time. Freedom involves having accountability, learning new disciplines, and choosing healthy habits. Whether instantaneous or over a period of time, it is the power of God that must set us free. Let us not fall into the trap of offering people a natural solution alone when they are looking for and need a supernatural one. Jesus came to set us free, and we are called to be free indeed. We need more than sin management. We need freedom from the grip of sin. His guidance and power provide a new way of living with Him and others.

Busyness

Although a relative of performance and "they can't make it without me," busyness has a subtle difference. It is the enslavement that keeps a person from being quiet with God and before God. The person who is a slave to busyness has to have their senses stimulated or has to be doing something all the time. This person can't find time to pray, spend time with God, or take a Sabbath. Downtime with family is hard to find. For some, silence is unnerving and must be replaced with conversation, music, or activity. And like Martha of the New Testament, busyness in the name of God is a great platform to criticize those who don't do enough, or who seem to be able to rest and find quiet time for God.

There were many factors that led to the extreme burnout I experienced and the self-destructive, sinful behavior that accompanied it. One symptom was being really poor at taking my weekly Sabbath day of rest and taking my vacation time each year. When I resigned from the church, I had been there eighteen years. The tracking of our Paid Time Off (PTO) had only been going on for about five years. In that short time, I had almost ten weeks of unused vacation time on the books.

Ironically, it took almost that amount of time to find a job. In that time, my body began to heal from years of overwork and unnecessary busyness. The clouds cleared as the summer progressed, and I was able to feel that rope loosen and fall off. Compulsive busyness can feel righteous and self-sacrificing, but it is still an enslaving practice. Trust me, it would be better for you to address this voluntarily before burnout and brokenness force it upon you. Don't buy the lie of this one. As the rope tightens, it suffocates your life, and you miss the balance and blessing of a life that knows when it is time to rest and renew. If you sense you are out of balance, here are a few ideas: turn off the phone, guard your day of rest each week, and have downtime with friends and family. Maybe you could practice silence so that you are comfortable with the quiet times. You want to be able to hear the whispers of the Holy Spirit and have the habit of knowing how to rest.

Crisis

Have you ever noticed how some aren't motivated unless there is some crisis? They artificially create deadlines by procrastinating. They make mountains out of molehills, which means small things become big when they don't have to. This is how some get motivated to be productive. In addition, there are those who want others to feel their crisis and conclude that if you aren't as worked up emotionally as they are, you must not care.

Being enslaved is both needing a crisis to motivate you or having to have others join you in crisis to validate their love and care for you. Whether you are the crisis maker or the crisis participant, it is an enslaving way to live. A healthy person will admit that life has enough naturally occurring drama, so that none of us have to artificially create it. An unhealthy person will try to define all crisis in their lives as naturally occurring without evaluating if that is really the case.

There are practices that help us sift out the artificially created crisis. You can choose to manage your time better so that you aren't always running late, rushing to meet deadlines at school or work, or feeling overwhelmed most of the time. You can choose to not work harder on someone's life than they are. You can choose to take responsibility for your choices but not the choices of others. The challenge with this area is that sometimes we don't want to live differently. We don't want to admit that the adrenaline of the urgent is the motivating drug we use to get things done. Sometimes we want to get sucked into the drama of others. I did this at different times in my life! You know what I finally had to admit? I wasn't as needed or as helpful as I thought to help the crisis-driven person. When I wasn't able to help someone anymore with their crisis, some moved on quite easily and found others who would enable their crisis-driven lifestyle. Some decided to look for a solution and became healthier. Either way, getting caught up in their crisis didn't help them or me.

With that said, there is a caveat in this. I concede there are uncaring people who ignore the needs of others when they could help in a healthy way. A person who ignores the needs of others could use the crisis-driven description to excuse the fact that they are truly callous and don't care about others that inconvenience their life. They justify being callous as having good boundaries. An uncaring spirit isn't what I am talking about here. I am talking about the person who needs to learn a healthy way to care. It is about the person who needs to discover boundaries that are healthy, necessary, and Biblical. God doesn't want us to use the crisis of life or the crisis of others to validate our existence, control others, or motivate ourselves to get something done.

Bitterness

I talked about this in its own chapter because it is the root of so much destruction in people's lives. It is listed here to remind us that bitterness is a deception from the pit of hell that will destroy your life and hurt those around you in untold ways. It will crush some and chase others away. It will leave you alone, hurting, angry, and inconsolable. It isn't a chain worth keeping. It only hurts you and others in the end.

Unhealthy Relationships

This can manifest itself in a variety of ways. One example of this is the family member or friend who insists on being the center of your universe. He or she insists on ranking above others, even God. Another example is the person who holds you captive by their critical spirit toward you. Or, it is the one who expects you to help them maintain their addiction while keeping its secret. Maybe it is the lazy person who expects you to rescue them from their troubles and emergencies, but is unwilling to do anything to help themselves. Some will let their life crash and then wait for someone to save the day or salvage the wreckage.

Although they can have different expressions, unhealthy relationships have a key identifier: one person trying to be valued most and another trying to prove that person is most valuable. If someone wants to be the god of your world, run. If they are consistently condemning or using guilt to motivate, stop giving in to it. If they aren't willing to participate in the solution to their problems, stop rescuing them. It isn't helping and it could be hurting them. Breaking free from unhealthy people and drawing boundaries can be hard. Some people exploit caring, compassionate people. Yet, each person chooses whether they let this happen to them. At some point, the right choice is to drop the chain connected to an unhealthy person. If they drop the chain as well, a new relationship can be built upon the right foundation. If not, you are responsible for choosing health for yourself, but you can't force someone else to do the same.

Their Failure Being the Excuse for Your Disobedience

Families fail. Churches fail. People fail. You fail. I fail. It is disappointing, hurtful, and can be disillusioning. But there are too many people letting the failure of others excuse their present disobedience. I can't count the number of people who stayed away from God and/or church because of a bad church experience. When we fail, pastors and parishioners alike must apologize for our sins and shortcomings. But letting someone's failure be your reason for years of disobedience to God hurts you and impacts your loved ones.

I am not trying to say letting go of the past is easy. Some pain is deep and excruciating. I had a close family member reject me in my youth and disown me as an adult. I carried the hole of this wound for years and didn't experience the deep healing until my forties. When you let someone's failure become your excuse, you let that person's sin and failure control your life. By doing so, you give Satan and his hordes ammunition to use as accusations and opportunities against you. This is not what God wants for you.

In addition, if you become hardened in an entrenched position of disobedience, you risk believing lies that this reactive behavior is acceptable. We have all been hurt in this life and, if we are honest, we have all hurt others as well. What we do after the hurts determines whether we walk the journey toward healing and freedom or fall into the trap of excusing our sin by pointing to the sin of others.

***

Remember, in the midst of a world of slaves, Jesus came to set us free. That includes everyone and anyone who will come to Him. That includes you. That includes me. That includes our enemies, those who have hurt us, and those who haven't. Whatever your place of brokenness and enslavement, Jesus paid the price for your freedom. Let the price he paid become the foundation of your freedom and break the chains that hold you down. As the songwriter said, "There is power in the name of Jesus, to break every chain!"

Chapter Nine

Forgiveness—Amazing and Complex

Forgiveness is both amazing and complex. It is amazing because God forgives in such a complete and unconditional way. By complex, I don't mean it is hard to understand God's forgiveness, because children can grasp it. I do mean that God worked through history, time, and space to come in the flesh and take the payment for sin and then rise from the dead. It is something only He could do, in a way only He could do it. Psalm 103:8-13 says:

> *The LORD is merciful and gracious,*
>
> *Slow to anger, and abounding in mercy.*
>
> *He will not always strive with us,*
>
> *Nor will He keep His anger forever.*
>
> *He has not dealt with us according to our sins,*
>
> *Nor punished us according to our iniquities.*
>
> *For as the heavens are high above the earth,*
>
> *So great is His mercy toward those who fear Him;*
>
> *As far as the east is from the west,*
>
> *So far has He removed our transgressions from us.*

Take this into account. God knows all about each and every sin we bring to Him as we seek forgiveness. Each hidden motive, our layers of intent, and the selfish manipulation that we tried to hide from others is exposed before Him. Hebrews 4:13 doesn't mince words as it describes Him as all-knowing: "And there is no creature hidden from His sight, but all things *are* naked and open to the eyes of Him to whom we *must give* account."

In the light of this, the words describing Him as being merciful and gracious are a relief. They are an oasis. For every sin we thought we committed in secret, He was present. He saw every action, knew every thought, heard every word, and discerned every motive. Even with this utterly complete knowledge of our depravity, He says that He is slow to anger and abounding in mercy. Even His anger and discipline aren't forever. It isn't some rant of blind rage and revenge. His discipline is loving. It is Him saying "enough," as a Father who loves us and everyone around us. Our sinful behavior violates His holiness, wounds others, and damages ourselves. He knows it needs to stop long before we are ready to admit it. Hebrews 12:5-1 teaches us that God's discipline is for our good and leads us to the beauty of His forgiveness and the fruit it produces in our lives.

My son, do not despise the chastening of the LORD,

Nor be discouraged when you are rebuked by Him;

For whom the LORD loves He chastens,

And scourges every son whom He receives.

If you endure chastening, God deals with you as with sons; for what son is there whom a father does not chasten? ⁸But if you are without chastening, of which all have become partakers, then you are illegitimate and not sons. Furthermore, we have had human fathers who corrected us, and we paid them respect. Shall we not much more readily be in subjection to the Father of spirits and live? For they indeed for a few days chastened us as seemed best to them, but He for our profit, that we may be partakers of His holiness. Now no chastening seems to be joyful for the present, but painful; nevertheless, afterward it yields the peaceable fruit of righteousness to those who have been trained by it.

This scripture declares that we can trust God to have our best in mind. God isn't inviting us to conclude that every struggle in life is the result of getting punished for our sin. It isn't whispering that everything is our fault and that we are scapegoats to be blamed. Remember, Jesus became the scapegoat for our sin, so that we could receive total forgiveness. This scripture is teaching us that God knows our deepest intent and is fully aware when we need correction to put us back on the path of His will for our lives. He doesn't buy our denials, sales pitches, or rationalizations. He isn't chased away by our self-condemnation and recriminations. He lovingly says, "Enough," and helps us get out of our way and stop being our own worst enemy. We can trust His discipline and what it will produce in our lives.

The LORD is merciful and gracious,

Slow to anger, and abounding in mercy.

He will not always strive with us,

Nor will He keep His anger forever.

He has not dealt with us according to our sins,

Nor punished us according to our iniquities.

For as the heavens are high above the earth,

So great is His mercy toward those who fear Him;

As far as the east is from the west,

So far has He removed our transgressions from us.

As a father pities his children,

So the Lord pities those who fear Him.

Psalm 103:8-13

It speaks to us that we haven't been punished as we deserve. God is redemptive, which means He paid the price to pave the road of forgiveness. It is a road we could never construct with our grandest intentions or good deeds. If we allow ourselves to come to the place of letting His Word and Spirit reveal to us the extent to which our sin is contrary to His perfect nature, it will give us a fear of Him and what we have done. But a good fear. Francis Chan talks about this in His video series "Basic." In it, he challenges the modern notion of redefining the fear of God into some mere respect. When he spoke of this dangerous revision of what the Scriptures actually say, I realized I need to be careful to not shortcut this vital teaching. It caused me to evaluate my sermons. I want people to know that God is approachable and that they can bring their sins and failures to Him. While this is completely true, it must also be balanced with the truth that when people saw God, they would fall on their faces before Him. Isaiah said in chapter 6 of the book with his name, "I am undone, a man of unclean lips." He saw God on His throne and believed He was finished. When we take Him at His Word, that our sin is an affront to Him, a violation of His sinless perfection, it will make us rightly afraid of the One and Only Great, Holy God who holds our lives in His hands.

But then, when we have a proper fear, God reveals He is our loving Father. He can be trusted and has provided a plan to forgive and redeem. Instead of seeing Him as less, we see Him as more, even though the fullness of His glory and nature won't be completely seen and comprehended until eternity. The truth of our sin placed before the perfection of His Being seems like the worst scenario. We deserve so much worse than we have gotten, yet He lifts us up and offers forgiveness. We ask for something that He has provided, something we can't earn or claim any shred of credit.

All we can do is lay ourselves before the God of the universe—the God of all things seen and unseen. And there, we discover His forgiveness. As far as the east is from the west, He casts our sin from us. East and west never meet. So, when God forgives, He considers the matter closed, done, never to be held against us or brought up again by Him. If we could just get a hold of the amazing words of Scripture, it would be a load lifted, leaving us awestruck at the amazing grace of God. Forgiveness would not be trite or common anymore. And it would change us.

Jesus spoke to this truth when He said of a woman He forgave, "Therefore I say to you, her sins, *which are* many, are forgiven, for she loved much. But to whom little is forgiven, *the same* loves little" (Luke 7:47). A woman who had been disgraced by her own sins received His forgiveness and became an example of love. Why? How else could she respond to the gift of her Savior? Love. It is amazing.

The other half of Jesus' statement is curious. How could anyone be forgiven "little"? The idea that someone has only been forgiven little speaks of the human bent toward comparison and contrast when it comes to sin. If I don't see my sin in light of God's holy, perfect nature, I can think I have been forgiven less than I have or less than others with whom I am comparing myself. It is in this type of deceptive thinking that one becomes a less loving person. When others become my rationale for justifying myself, they become less than me (from my self-righteous perspective), and I develop a condescending, condemning spirit toward others.

If, on the other hand, I see the extent of my sin and the amazing gift of His forgiveness, it makes me loving. "We love Him because He first loved us" is what 1 John 4:19 says. You and I can respond to the brokenness and sin of others with love. Not a love, mind you, that doesn't see their sin or excuses it away, but rather a love that sees God's forgiveness as greater than their sin, just as it was greater than our sin.

We can't give someone an end run around the needed brokenness before God because of their sin. We can see the real enemies (sin and Satan) and the real Redeemer of this situation (Jesus Christ). Although there is legal justice in this life for some sins, understanding God's forgiveness can keep us from being bound up with a need for revenge. We can see life through the lens of His forgiveness. It is truly an amazing gift. We know it because He has said it, lived it, and provided the way for it. Some of us know it because we have experienced it. His Word is true regardless if I experience it, but I am grateful that all of us can experience its Truth personally, and that this experience brings His Word alive within us.

We need this gift. It liberates us before God. It helps us deal with the domino effect of our sin in the natural world of human memory and human consequences. You and I tend to remember sin. We can remember our own sin to the point of struggling to forgive ourselves. Or, we remember the sins of others to the point of being unable to forgive them.

When we sin, others see our sin as well. There can be disappointment, broken trust, and at times, a hard road back with others. When you confess your sin to God, He sees your heart and if you are sincere and mean it. When you do, He pours out forgiveness and washes away your guilt before Him and for eternity. The challenge is that others can't see the intention of our heart, just as we can't see theirs. It has to be observed over the course of time, in behavior, words, and attitudes. When we hurt others by our sin, they may feel duped because they trusted us. We violated that trust and then blindsided them with our sin. Our intent was veiled until it came out like a knockout punch that lifted them off their feet. The same happens to us when we are blindsided by other people's sin as well.

This is one reason forgiveness with people is different than with God. Often people are hesitant to forgive. How do they know whether or not the intent of our heart and mind has changed? We fooled them before. What keeps us from doing it again? As a result, many watch, wait, question, prod, doubt, wonder, cautiously hope, or cynically wait. Before we get frustrated by all of this and tell people to get over it, let's remember we can and probably have done the same thing with others when we have been hurt by their sin.

In this cycle, we are reduced to suspiciously circling each other, wondering if we can get close again. Some decide it isn't worth it. At times, the frequency of the haymakers of sin have been so damaging, people decide they have to get away from unpredictable people for the safety of themselves and their loved ones. Simply put, forgiveness with others is more complex. So, how can we let the fear of God and the forgiveness of God integrate into how we respond to others when it comes to sin and forgiveness?

First, don't let your decision of forgiveness be dependent on someone else's response. You pay the price when forgiveness becomes an "if they do 'x,' then I will" proposition. The other person has control of the situation when you make the decision to forgive based on whether or not they ask for it, change, apologize, or meet your standards. When any of us fall into this trap of unforgiveness, our obedience to God is dependent on another person's obedience. What happens if they never choose to listen to God and His Word? What if they never think they did wrong? We end up poisoned with bitterness and hyper-focusing on someone else's sins rather than keeping our eyes on the Lord and listening to Him. When this happens, it puts their sin above the redemptive work of Christ in our lives. This type of misery is never God's will for anyone, even though many choose it.

If, on the other hand, we have a clear picture of what Jesus Christ has done for us, then it can change how we respond to the sins of others. He paid a debt for us that dwarfs any debt someone else has in their account with us. Think about this as you consider the extent to which humanity expresses evil and hatefulness toward each other. There are people who are calculated as they commit violent sexual sin, grotesque murder, and exploit the weak with wanton cruelty. In light of the horrors committed by humanity, it could lead you to ask, "How could my sin be such an affront to God when others have done so much worse than me?"

When it comes to God, the standard isn't my sin versus others' sin. It is my sin compared with the Holy God of the universe. In His presence, measured against His standard, I am so far in debt, I can't see the top of the pit I have dug. In light of that, the sin committed against me pales in comparison. This way of thinking can seem insulting and offensive to some because of the extent to which others have sinned against them. But this isn't about their sin. It is about who God is and what He wants for your life. He wants you to be free and see yourself clearly in His sight. He wants you to see His gift and the immeasurable love He shows as He gives it. As you receive this gift and live in His love and grace, He calls you to live with that as your benchmark on how to respond to others. This isn't a call to let people get away with deeds that should be accounted for in this life. It is a call to not let their evil control your life.

Matthew 18:21-35 recounts Jesus' description of how we were to respond to others' sin:

> *Then Peter came to Him and said, "Lord, how often shall my brother sin against me, and I forgive him? Up to seven times?"*
>
> *Jesus said to him, "I do not say to you, up to seven times, but up to seventy times seven. Therefore the kingdom of heaven is like a certain king who wanted to settle accounts with his servants. And when he had begun to settle accounts, one was brought to him who owed him ten thousand talents. But as he was not able to pay, his master commanded that he be sold, with his wife and children and all that he had, and that payment be made. The servant therefore fell down before him, saying, "Master, have patience with me, and I will pay you all." Then the master of that servant was moved with compassion, released him, and forgave him the debt.*
>
> *But that servant went out and found one of his fellow servants*

101

who owed him a hundred denarii; and he laid hands on him and took him by the throat, saying, "Pay me what you owe!" So his fellow servant fell down at his feet and begged him, saying, "Have patience with me, and I will pay you all." And he would not, but went and threw him into prison till he should pay the debt. So when his fellow servants saw what had been done, they were very grieved, and came and told their master all that had been done. Then his master, after he had called him, said to him, "You wicked servant! I forgave you all that debt because you begged me. Should you not also have had compassion on your fellow servant, just as I had pity on you?" And his master was angry, and delivered him to the torturers until he should pay all that was due to him. "So My heavenly Father also will do to you if each of you, from his heart, does not forgive his brother his trespasses."

Some struggle with this and protest. "Forgiveness is something that someone asks for! If they don't acknowledge wrongdoing, how can I forgive? Do I act like nothing happened if they never take responsibility for their offense?" Here is a vital key. Forgiveness isn't saying what someone did is alright or acceptable. It is saying that their sin won't have control over your life. Forgiveness is making a distinction between your relationship with God and your relationship with others.

Someone's callous disregard may require you to change the boundaries of the relationship. Sometimes it is best to have distance for the sake of your safety and the safety of your loved ones. An abused spouse is not expected to stay in proximity of the abuser to demonstrate forgiveness. The abused is called to forgive so that they aren't prisoners on the inside, even as they are set free on the outside. Is forgiveness a journey for most of us? Yes. It is committing to obey God even when we don't feel it, want it, or understand it. In time, our feelings will catch up with the obedience, rather than having our feelings control our obedience. Jimmy Evans talks about this topic in great detail in his sermons and writings as he and his wife minister to thousands of married couples every year. It sure helped Barb and me as we healed from the great sins I committed against her and our marriage. Forgiveness is a gift that must be given not just received. Jimmy says repeatedly, "Forgiveness doesn't make them right. It makes you free."

This is mindboggling when you think of atrocities and genocide that has taken place throughout history. My mother's side of the family is Jewish, and when I lived across the river from Washington D.C., I spent time at the Holocaust Museum. I visited and did some research. It was staggering to consider the millions of Jewish men, women, and children that died at the hands of unspeakable evil. As I studied and reflected on this staggering loss of innocent lives, I pray that humanity will learn its lessons and never repeat this indescribable evil, and if they cross the line, that the rule of law holds them accountable. Yet, as I think about this time, I also reflected on the writings of Victor Frankl, who survived the Holocaust, yet spoke so eloquently and powerfully of forgiveness. He decided he wouldn't let his captors decide who he was going to be on the inside. His story is inspiring. I recalled the writing of Corrie Ten Boom, who also walked the journey of forgiveness of those who killed her family in the Holocaust, after they were caught hiding and protecting Jewish people who were being hunted down by the Nazis. Her family did what was right, yet they suffered and sacrificed for this righteousness. Years after the war, Corrie wrote about speaking one night and having a former guard at the concentration camp come up to her and ask forgiveness. She gave it, which is amazing when you consider her losses.

Forgiveness doesn't mean justice in this life is overlooked or ignored. The rule of law, justly applied, is a critical foundation of any democratic society. When evil people murder and destroy, they should be held accountable before the justice systems of this world. Forgiveness isn't glossing over what someone has done. Forgiveness recognizes that the evil, no matter how heinous, shouldn't hold sway over one's life. It is easier to talk about it than it is to live it, but it is God's invitation to us, nonetheless. I am just scratching the surface of a topic that deals with deep hurts, but I ask you to consider if the sins of others are strings still attached to your life.

Before I close this chapter, let's speak for a moment about the times when you and I are the ones needing to seek forgiveness from someone else. There are moments we can't point the finger and ask God why the other person did what they did. Instead, we look in the mirror and wonder how we did what we did. We arrived at places of sin and pigpens of self-destruction, and others have been damaged in the wake of our actions. Even if you want to fix it, you can't force healing on those you have hurt. So now what? I offer you three thoughts on this.

First, *pursue forgiveness humbly.* As you ask for it, don't give disclaimers or excuses. Be clear and honest about how your sin affected someone else and be willing to let them tell you how it affected them. Do be careful, in your sense of guilt, to avoid details that can plague someone's memories long term. When I walked through the forgiveness journey with Barb over my emotional and physical affair, I avoided details of places and specifics that wouldn't help healing. Because I had hid my sin for months after I had stopped committing it, she found out through another and heard details that made it much harder on her than if she had heard from me first.

When confronted, I did confess and come clean, but I also saw how details shared by another devastated her. I knew that as we moved forward, I had the responsibility not to add unneeded details that would hinder healing long after forgiveness had been granted. We sought the help of a Christian counselor who was trained and experienced on helping us set these boundaries to help healing. I had to share more details than I wanted, and Barb chose to hear less details than she would have chosen for the sake of her healing.

Second, *you need to be patient.* As the offending party, you can't control, manipulate, or rush someone else's forgiveness journey. Remember, our loved ones or friends are walking this journey because of sin we committed. We are not the victims here. Even though it is hard, and we want to move forward, don't force another's journey. Be willing to get counseling, listen to their pain, and wait for it. How is this possible? Well, the final point gives the power for this.

Live in light of God's forgiveness even while your relationships with others are still healing. Be secure in your identity in Him. Because He forgives out of His limitless love, perfect promises, and amazing grace, He can lift you back up, straighten your back, and put joy back into your life. You don't have to wait to get up until others give you permission. You do have to submit under human accountability to demonstrate a changed life. You don't have to wait for their permission on the outside to have peace on the inside. This isn't thumbing your nose at their pain. It is resting in His belief in you because He knows your heart and motives. He forgives and then chooses to forget. It is because of His limitless power and love that

He can do this. Others need time and power from God to heal. Don't condemn them for not being God. Be grateful for who He is, even while you walk the journey with people.

***

Remember, no one else can see into your deepest places like God can. Others have to observe it over time as His forgiveness in you and His grace upon you comes spilling out into the realm they can see. Pursue this humbly, wait patiently, and be anchored in Him. Forgiveness can be complex with each other, but with God it is amazing! Whether you face issues connected with past glory days, regrets over missed opportunities, or pain from your past or others' past, forgiveness is an essential part of healing. It is God's gift to us, for us, and even through us. Let's commit to share His amazing gift with each other.

Chapter Ten

Responding to the Accident Scene

The Front Range of Colorado has a major interstate running north/ south. It is our Interstate 25. Running from Canada to Mexico, it is a major trucking route that intersects Interstate 70 and Interstate 40 respectively.

For those of us in Colorado Springs, the sixty or so miles from our city to downtown Denver is essential. There are commuters that have bought homes in the northern part of our city who work in Denver. They trade a long commute for being able to take Denver wages to purchase homes in the Colorado Springs housing market. There are hordes of Broncos fans, who use the highway to fill Mile High Stadium with 75,000 fans at home games.

And as one of the small number of American cities with the five major professional sports, people also drive I-25 to route for the Rockies (MLB), Avalanche (NHL), Nuggets (NBA), and the Rapids (MLS). There are days in the fall when baseball is still in season, football has started, and on occasions when the Rockies make the playoffs. It can even stretch into preseason basketball and hockey. There have been times that over 100,000 people have been on Interstate 25 at one time within miles of the downtown sporting venues.

Besides that, Colorado is the home to some of the greatest outdoor options in the nation. Dozens of "Fourteeners" rise up as part of the Rocky Mountains. For those who don't know, a "fourteener" is a mountain at least 14,000 feet high. There are 40+ of them in Colorado between 14,000-15,000 feet. Thousands of people come during the various hunting seasons throughout the fall. In the warmer months, there are the campers, white-water rafters, and fishermen of all types. From Memorial Day until Labor Day, good luck driving fast on Interstate 25 from Friday-Sunday.

When the leaves turn their fall colors in late September and early October, I-25 is full of people connecting to westward highways going to see Aspens' golden colors. When the snow falls, cars travel to their favorite slopes to snowboard and ski. Most weekends from Thanksgiving through spring break, I-25 stays very busy. Finally, there are the tractor trailers by the thousands that use I-25 daily as a hub for commerce and industry. It is an interstate worthy of wide-open spaces and the great expanse of our majestic state.

That is until you get caught in a traffic jam leading up to an accident scene. Once you leave the metropolis of Denver (four lanes each way) and the mid-size city of Colorado Springs (three lanes each way), most of I-25 is a four-lane interstate. In fact, the twenty-five mile stretch between Monument and Castle Rock is notorious for backing up for miles from one accident. This stretch is between Denver and Colorado Springs, so there is a high volume of vehicles using this four-lane stretch. When the snow hits fast, it can become a treacherous ice rink. When summer thunderstorms roll over the mountains, visibility drops and wet roads can catch aggressive drivers by surprise. Even on a perfect day of sun and blue skies, drivers going too fast (way above the 75 mph speed limit) can get in accidents that turn I-25 into a parking lot. People inch along until they come upon the accident scene. Many express relief they weren't in it. Some pray for those who were, and others curiously look on as they pass by. Once they pass the scene though, it is full speed ahead.

As you reflect on the word picture I drew, you probably see where I am going. Accident scenes happen in life, and I'm not talking about the ones on highways. The issues of glory days, regrets over missed opportunities, and past pain can be significant factors in having a wreck on the highway of life. One moment, you were cruising along, and then unexpectedly, life becomes a mangled wreck. If this happens to you, or has happened to you, the response you choose in the aftermath will greatly impact the direction of your life. We all have to decide on what to do with our accident scenes -

the places where we wrecked our lives or had someone else crash into us. After challenging you for many chapters to let God do surgery on your life and reveal its sinful and/or broken places, it is time to talk about the time when God calls you to get up and get back into life.

Like I-25, you are full of great potential. When operating according to Design, you can be a sight to behold, but when life gets backed up by your accidents, whether through ignorance, intention, or impact from others, it can be a mess. Although accidents can be gruesome at times, they are meant to be cleaned up, and traffic is supposed to resume to posted speeds. Although this is the intended goal, the cleanup process can be hindered by the onlookers. On the highways, or in an individual's life, I like the term "rubberneckers."

You may have different names for them in your part of the world, but all the terms refer to the same type of people. It is those who take too long to check out an accident as they drive by. They can slow traffic longer, cause other accidents, and needlessly delay the recovery process. I-25 isn't the only place you find these people. They are found all around us every day, and they are magnetically drawn to people who have failed and fallen, both to the victims and victimizers. I have found that a minority of them are helpful. I thank God for this encouraging group, but most "rubberneckers" hinder and hold back. If you are going to get up and get back into life as God intends, you must be able to identify the good ones and sift out the rest.

God wants you to get up, live in His forgiveness, and stop wallowing at your accident scene. You can't wait for others to give you permission to get up. There are first responders in our lives who intervene so we can get up. With the Holy Spirit as the Ultimate First Responder, He can also work through pastors and counselors, family and friends, doctors and nurses, prophets and evangelists, helpers and healers. These guide us on the path to healing and restoration. Many of the remaining "rubberneckers" have no interest in your healing. They just like to check out your accident scene. There comes a point when you need to stop being someone else's spectacle. Let's talk for a bit on how you can discern on your highway how to distinguish those out for your good and those who are not. The ones who aren't needed to move on for everyone's good, especially yours. The following categories will help you identify them.

108

Obsessive

This is the person who always seems to be the self-proclaimed expert at the accident scene, except their professed expertise doesn't seem to do any good. They always seem ready to give a correction or change for others or give a criticism that discourages. Ironically, they tend to give themselves a pass. They may not come right out and say how good they are, but you have a hard time remembering them talk about lessons they learned from their own failures and shortcomings. Their cycle is to obsessively look for the fault in others as a way of creating a platform to proclaim their expertise. The person who failed, by ignorance or intention, is just someone to be used as an opportunity to "toot" their own horn. They make themselves big by keeping others small. This is not the type of first responder you want in your corner. The expertise doesn't lead to encouragement or a hopeful path on how to move forward. Hope and encouragement would set you free, and that isn't the goal of the obsessive critic. Keeping you down or believing that you need them is what drives the obsessive critic.

Impersonator

Just like there is peril in getting fooled by someone impersonating a police officer, there is danger in this "would-be helper." The one who poses as a police officer uses the position of trust to gain access to someone's home or information in order to exploit them. When a person has an accident scene in life, the impersonator looks caring like a first responder, but their intention isn't so benevolent. They just want access to the accident scene of your life so that you will trust them with all the gory details of the story of your pain or failure. In the season of facing one's sin and wrongdoing, the impersonator can look like they care in order to gain temporary trust, but once they have heard all the juicy tidbits, they are nowhere to be found. Once they are "in the know," they go. A true first responder will stay the course, call you to a journey of healing and hard work but make the decision to stick it out once the headlines fade. Your mountaintops reveal your fans. Valleys reveal your friends.

Critical Spirit

This is different from the obsessive person in that they don't have to know you to be critical of you. They are the armchair quarterback who criticizes others from a distance, but can be loud enough to be heard. Using the driving analogy, they are the ones who drive by the accident scene and focus on condemning the bad driving of others, while smugly holding to their own rightness. While the obsessive person wants to stay in your life to keep you down, the critical spirit just wants to use you as an object lesson of badness while they can only see their own goodness, with little or no relationship required to do it. They just need a drive by to point out to others what a mess you are.

Celebrator

Think of a time when you were driving on the highway and a car blew past you going way over the speed limit. Later you come across that car and they are either pulled over by the police or you see the smashed metal of their accident. A celebrator gets joy and satisfaction out of others getting what they think they deserve. They are much less likely to celebrate the success of others around them as they are to celebrate the punishment of others. Others do wrong things, and sometimes that person is me or you or others. But I ask, what good is it when you face the consequences of failure to have someone in your life who gets a perverse joy out of it? In this person's hope of seeing justice meted out, one can be justified in confronting injustice but have a perverse joy over punishment.

While we should all stand up to injustice, there is a sniff test we need to pass. Do I have a burden for injustice in the world when it has no impact on me or those I know? In other words, is my passion to confront injustice only aroused when wrongdoing affects me personally, or is there a genuine heart for others when I have nothing to gain from the right thing being done? The celebrator tends to be wrapped up in the injustice that is personal. Thus, when they see punishment happen, it is a vindication that they were wronged, and someone got punished for it. This isn't the healthiest person to have in your sphere of influence at an accident scene. When it doesn't have anything to do with them, they tend not to care. When they are connected to it, your punishment brings them too much pleasure.

Reporter

I write this eight days before the 2016 presidential election. I tell you this for the sake of context. Along with millions of others, I have just watched for months as candidates complain about the media with great inconsistency. On one hand, if they aren't getting enough coverage, the media is biased against them by giving the opposing side more attention and reporting time. On the other hand, if the media pays too much attention to them and asks them about their words and deeds, then it is a conspiracy meant to tilt the election toward their opponent. Both sides have been guilty. They want a press protected by free speech, as long as the free speech is agreeable to them and about them.

That's kind of the rub with free speech. You don't get to control it. Each person has the right to speak what he/she wants, as long as it doesn't incite or influence criminal behavior (e.g., crowd/mob violence, child pornography). With the right of free speech, there is also a responsibility. Our words are not expressed in a vacuum. They are in the context of our daily lives. So, a person has the right to post a late-night Facebook rant about someone or something that enrages them, but the next day, when the morning fog has cleared with the second cup of coffee, the relational backlash can be a reality. If dozens or hundreds of people saw it, it's a bit idealistic to sit back bewildered on why a relationship is in crisis or complain that people are venting their opinions back at you. Free speech has its consequences. It is a right with a responsibility. Am I advocating restricting free speech? No. I am saying we should stop being so impulsive about our words (print or spoken). Instead, we should think our words through and evaluate each situation with clear heads. How does all this connect to this chapter? Glad you asked.

When I had to step down as pastor of the local church I served for eighteen years, it was tied to poor, sinful decisions I made after ignoring years of burnout and bitterness. I chose self-reliance and secrecy. I did not seek help when I should have, so now

111

accountability and help was in the form of an intervention. Although I didn't have to share details with hundreds of people in one moment, I wasn't absolved from having to be accountable. Having spent my adult life in a position of trust and public leadership, there was a season of reporting, so to speak. I had to confess my sin to God, my wife, each of my four kids, my superintendent, and my local board. Then, over the next year, a couple of hundred people were talked to as well. Most of these conversations happened one on one or with a couple, but there were a couple of group settings. It was a consequence that was humiliating, exhausting, and painful. It was a legitimate consequence for my sin. No self-pity. Publicly, I had to resign and explain that there were behaviors from my burnout that required me to be done immediately. After eighteen years at the same church, I was done on a single day.

But that didn't mean I had to share the details with everyone who wanted to know. There were "reporters" who only wanted to know so they could tell others. That's a nice way of referring to gossips. When your life has an accident scene due to your failure or sin, there is a ripple effect of reporting that is normal and necessary. You have to face the music. Avoid ranting on those people who were hurt by your sin. They deserve an accounting for what you did and a genuine apology. That being said, you can draw the line on those whose intent is nothing more than to spread the news of your collision as a tawdry piece of news. You do have to be accountable. You don't have to expose yourself to dangerous, malicious people.

Carfax

This is the report that tells you about the history of a car before you purchase it. Specifically, it tells you if the car has had chronic problems or if it has been in an accident. Sometimes a car can be fixed up enough to hide core issues that make it a bad deal. While this is great for car buying, beware of those historians who view you as permanently damaged goods. If you choose not to repent to God and others, your sin and its poison will stay with you. If you don't submit under Biblical accountability and the journey of restoring trust and wholeness, you can repeat cycles of destruction.

If, on the other hand, you let God transform your life, and you actively participate in the process with consistency and commitment, you don't have to be marked as permanently damaged

112

goods. Stay away from those who try to convince you otherwise. It is an amazing miracle of God's mercy when He says our sin is "cast as far as the east is from the west" or "cast into the depths of the sea." He isn't a historian. With people, it takes time to rebuild relationships and earn trust. Our lives must demonstrate change over the course of time. But as you submit to a healing journey, reject the notion that your past is the final report on your life. It is true that not all relationships are healed. You can't always go back and live the same life you had. You can move forward, however, and know that there is a future in which your past isn't the final word on your life and God's plan for you.

The Good Ones

After all these red-flag categories, you may be wondering who is left at the accident scene. It seems as though I have counseled you to chase just about everyone away. Well, not quite. This chapter is not a rant against the world. It is a call to stop looking back when it is time to move forward. We must confront the reality of our sin and address the need of forgiveness through the blood of Jesus Christ. We must commit to the journey of healing. We need to deal with the repercussions of the sin and brokenness we chose or experienced at the hand of others. As we do, we can find there are merciful healers and helpers at the accident scene.

We discover the Great Healer and Lover of our Soul is our Heavenly Father. One drop of His Son's blood is greater than all the sin we have committed and all the sin committed against us. Moving forward isn't rebelling against the necessary work of restoration, but moving forward is a gift that comes from the miracle of God's love for us. Jimmy Evans spoke about restoration powerfully in a sermon my wife and I listened to one morning as we were walking through our healing journey. He said, "Miracles are instantaneous. Restoration is a lifestyle." We partner with God and trust Him in the healing process. He has done all the heavy lifting through His Son and His Spirit, but He does give us a responsibility to respond as He instructs us and submit to Him and "good ones" He puts in our lives.

These "good ones" are those God puts in your life that help with the restoring and healing process. As they point you toward the life God has for you in the future, these people avoid enslaving you to the problems of the past. Counselors, pastors, and certain family and friends may rightfully challenge us to understand how the past affected others so we see its impact more clearly. They may have to confront us to reject old lies and lifestyles that would perpetuate the past into the future. It is a necessary part of accountability. It requires us being teachable, humble, and living out a heart of repentance. At their heart though, the "good ones" at the accident scene agree with God's plan to heal, restore, and release His great power into our lives. They want the fullness of His blessings and plan for our lives. They want to see us living in our identity in Jesus Christ through the power of the Holy Spirit. They want us to get up and move forward.

The Good Ones will call us to be well and not be perpetually identified with our past sin, sickness, and broken mindsets. This is the will of God for your life, and this freedom is why Jesus Christ came into the world—to die on a cross and rise from the dead. Isaiah 61 is a Messianic passage that spoke of the ministry of Jesus Christ centuries before He left heaven to come into our world. It speaks of His power to heal and His plan to save and restore. As you read it, be mindful of what His will is for you, even if you have crashed in your life. The carnage laying at your feet isn't your destiny. I urge to stand up in the name of Jesus Christ. Trust in His power to save, heal, and restore. It is time to get up with God and others on the journey to wholeness in Him and to restoration with others. It is time to be healed and move forward. Let the promises and expectant hope of this passage speak into your life today.

"The Spirit of the Lord GOD is upon Me,
Because the LORD has anointed Me
To preach good tidings to the poor;
He has sent Me to heal the brokenhearted,
To proclaim liberty to the captives,
And the opening of the prison to those who are bound;
To proclaim the acceptable year of the LORD,
And the day of vengeance of our God;
To comfort all who mourn,
To console those who mourn in Zion,
To give them beauty for ashes,
The oil of joy for mourning,
The garment of praise for the spirit of heaviness;
That they may be called trees of righteousness,
The planting of the LORD, that He may be glorified."
And they shall rebuild the old ruins,

114

They shall raise up the former desolations,
And they shall repair the ruined cities,
The desolations of many generations.
Strangers shall stand and feed your flocks,
And the sons of the foreigner
Shall be your plowmen and your vinedressers.
But you shall be named the priests of the LORD,
They shall call you the servants of our God.
You shall eat the riches of the Gentiles,
And in their glory you shall boast.
Instead of your shame you shall have double honor,
And instead of confusion they shall rejoice in their portion.
Therefore in their land they shall possess double;
Everlasting joy shall be theirs.
"For I, the LORD, love justice;
I hate robbery for burnt offering;
I will direct their work in truth,
And will make with them an everlasting covenant.
Their descendants shall be known among the Gentiles,
And their offspring among the people.
All who see them shall acknowledge them,
That they are the posterity whom the LORD has blessed."
I will greatly rejoice in the LORD,
My soul shall be joyful in my God;
For He has clothed me with the garments of salvation,
He has covered me with the robe of righteousness,
As a bridegroom decks himself with ornaments,
And as a bride adorns herself with her jewels.
For as the earth brings forth its bud,
As the garden causes the things that are sown in it to spring forth,
So the Lord GOD will cause righteousness and praise to spring forth before
all the nations.

Chapter Eleven

He's the Winner! Victory Is Mine!

I spent my whole life striving for victory. Whether it was in sports, marriage, school, career, parenting, or just about any endeavor, winning and/or success was my goal. There are healthy and unhealthy sides to that kind of drive. As a father, I have watched my kids emulate these qualities, sometimes for the good and other times, not so. My youngest son, Ben, has always been competitive, just like me. From the time of being a toddler, we could see this burning desire to win. As a five-year-old, he would cry out, "I am the winner! Victory is mine!" for just about any type of victory.

As we would walk to our car in any parking lot, he would wait for the signal that it was safe enough for him to run ahead of us. His goal was to touch the car first. It was amusing to watch his unbridled joy to beat the rest of us to the car and go into his celebration. His three older siblings would smile, amused at his desire to win. Sometimes, his sister would purposely beat him to the car and cry out his same phrase, "I am the winner! Victory is mine!" At five years old, Ben didn't take defeat very well. He would protest with tears and say in a protesting tone, "NO! I am the winner!" We had to work with him on sportsmanship as he grew to understand that none of us wins all the time. Now he has a healthy desire to win and an ability to lose much more graciously. He loves to win, but he loves people more. Atta boy, Ben.

As he grew, we also had to help him see that some things weren't worth competing to win. Even competitive people can come to understand that not everything is a contest with winners and losers. As we drove Ben to preschool and kindergarten, he would urge us to pass the car in front of us because he wanted to "beat them." It was interesting to attempt to describe this notion that when you are driving, there is always someone ahead of you. Granted, some of you have driven on roads with people who never quite learned this premise. For instance, there is the driver who goes under the speed limit until you start to pass, and then decides it's time to speed up. He realizes he is about to lose his position and resists you "winning." Once you pass him, he stays up with you for a while but then returns to driving slower. Many of you have been there. If you don't know what I am talking about, you might be that driv.. . Uh, never mind. Back to my son before I get into much trouble. It took months to convince him that we didn't need to pass the cars in front of us. Imagine how many days he needlessly felt like he had lost the race to school.

Well, he's not the only human being who spent unnecessary time feeling like he has lost. At least Ben will be able to give a reasonable defense when we smile and tell this family story. He can say, "I was five years old." I, on the other hand, don't have such a reason that gives a rational explanation on why I spent decades trying to win something that was never meant to be a competition. It may not have been cars on the road (most of the time), but it sure was most everything else. Driven by a need to prove my worth to myself, others, and even God, I was driven by insecurities and an unhealthy need for success that would someone prove my worth. Like Ben's view of the cars, I wasn't willing to recognize I was competing for something that wasn't meant to be a competition. The problem with me is that I was adult, and not a five-year-old.

In marriage, I wanted to prove I could be the best husband and beat back the fears of divorce that stemmed from coming from a divorced home. I genuinely wanted to love and serve Barb and give her a life that she would describe as the best she could have wished for. The problem was that I was driven by my own picture of what that ideal victory would look like and was quite defensive when she would try and tell me what she needed. When a man says, "I am a good husband" to his wife, it misses the mark. Shouldn't she have a say in how I was doing? For years, I didn't see this. I really thought she should get a clearer picture that she had a husband who was working his guts out trying to please her. A little appreciation sure would have been nice. Yeah, I was that guy.

When I heard a sermon by Jimmy Evans on this cycle of broken behavior, it was a dose of cold water that cleared out the cobwebs. He said matter of fact, "Your spouse is the one who tells you whether or not you are a good spouse." Now that changes things, and truth of it hit me between the eyes. Foolishly, I had been trying to declare victory when marriage wasn't ever meant to be a competition. Instead, I should have been listening to Barb talk and let her communicate what her needs were. Although I would serve her according to her love language (acts of service), it was driven by an inner need for recognition and affirmation. When she didn't say thank you or express enough timely gratitude, I would get grumpy or pout about her not being a thankful person.

It may seem odd that I spent so much time missing the obvious, but a skewed view of victory can do that to a person. Unfortunately, others can suffer and be hurt when this happens. Our marriage counselor addressed this when he observed that I had a hard time letting anyone say anything positive about me because I didn't think I deserved it or was skeptical the other person was sincere. Yet, I still had a deep need for approval. It was a recipe for misery, and trust me, the stew never tasted right. In addition to marriage, the drive for competitive success came out in parenting, ministry, friendship, and even in my casual athletic pursuits. This need for victory continued in some form or another into my forties.

When I make these disclosures, I am not trying to "win" at being transparent. Trust me, I had enough shame and regret over people who were hurt. There have been opportunities lost, and negative impressions were left on people about what it means to serve God and be a spiritual leader. Letting that dirt get swept under the rug wouldn't bother me in the least. I have no desire to win at this. It is my hope that if you are willing to hear parts of my story, you may be willing to ponder yours. And if you are willing to ponder your story, maybe you will be willing to ask some hard questions of yourself and listen to others who interact with you. I pray you choose to do this.

Are there roles and relationships in your life where you feel you have to win? Do you have an unhealthy need to be the center of attention? How do you conduct yourself in areas of approval, such as finances, parenting, marriage, work, or resolving conflict? Are you

118

running a race to try to escape your past regrets, hurts, and sins? Have you made faulty conclusions about yourself, others, or God after traumatic moments? Do you have a need to get the final word or have the better story, in effect, "one upping" someone in a conversation?

Do you need to prove how much you know? Do you feed a need or desire to get attention from others in unhealthy ways? Are you grappling with a sense of failure that leaks out as a frustration and anger over where you are in life? Does criticism seem devastating because you have tied your identity so closely to key roles (parenting, marriage, work) that you can't receive constructive correction? Do you tend to "steamroll" others out of a blinded need to "win" on your terms? Are people in your life a means to an end? Do you want more from people than for people? While this not an exhaustive list, I think you get the point. Most of us could identify with at least one of those questions. If you are trying to win at things that were never meant to be won, what could be a healthy next step?

A good place to start is figuring out if there is something or someone that was lost in the past, which you could be trying to make up for in the present. If you lost or never had the approval of a parent, you can chase after accolades and achievement for years. Strangely, for most it will never ring true or give the peace you seek because it isn't solving the core problem. Maybe you lost someone to death or a deep rejection, like divorce. In response, you might try to win at building walls of protection in your life. You could try to win at being mad at God for the suffering you have experienced. Maybe you lost self-confidence when others mocked you, condemned you, or made you the scapegoat for their problems. Did you lose a sense of innocence and identity when someone abused you sexually or physically?

Whatever the loss, it is real, and it could be affecting you today. If it is, healthy healing and supernatural help from God needs to take place. If you are trying to achieve victory in another area to make up for that loss, you never feel like you win. It's like trying to feed an animal that never gets full. Many counselors, pastors, teachers, and social workers can tell you a story of an indelible moment of pain in their lives that motivated them to want to help others from the same type of hurt. While wanting to be an instrument of healing, help, and empowerment is a deep calling, being able to sort through one's past is key to maximizing effectiveness and personal contentment. We don't want to be serving others while being unaware of our own blind spots. The crashes from those blind spots could negatively impact someone else's future.

Frankly, we are all on a journey, and none of us are perfect. There is good news though. When we mess up, God forgives, and often so do others. God's will, after forgiveness, is to bring you to a place where He can work through you and not in spite of you. So, let me offer you some principles and practices that can help you discern where you are, where you have been, and where God wants to lead you.

Admit you don't know as much as you think you do. I am talking about being humble before the key people in your life. There is freedom in not having to try to prove how much you know. The knowledge you do have can be for others rather than trying to satisfy an unquenchable thirst for approval. There is great freedom in learning to say the words, "I don't know." It isn't failure, even though it may temporarily feel like it.

Be teachable. This is more than being self-taught. I spent far too many years dismissing my wife's request that we get marriage counseling. I was scared I didn't know enough and thought I could self-diagnose and then self-correct the areas I needed to address. Being self-taught isn't bad in all situations. It can be good and demonstrate you are a resourceful and determined problem solver, but if you can't submit under someone else's leadership and instruction, you prevent learning some of the deeper lessons of life that aren't learned when you go solo. Now that Barb and I have walked with a skilled helper, I wish I would have done this years earlier.

Carefully choose who you let influence your life. Out of a need for approval, I let certain people have an undue influence who really didn't have my best interests at heart. They sure had their interests at heart. It led to a roller coaster ride of trying to be the sum of the parts everyone wanted me to be. Over the long haul, it was a faulty way of living. Most were nowhere to be found when I ceased to serve their purposes and goals. I let the wrong people in and kept the wrong people out. For those who tend to keep others out, make sure you aren't alienating the very people who love you and want the best for you. And if you tend to let the wrong people in, or too many people in, reducing or changing who you let in is key. As you choose who to let in, make sure you let God have His rightful place as Lord of your life. It isn't His fault when other people hurt you. Letting Him in is the key step to true healing.

Determine to learn that your ultimate value doesn't come from what you do. It comes from who you are and Whose you are. It sounds simple, but it can be hard to practice. To understand this, we need the Truth that comes from outside of ourselves. And by outside of yourself, I mean the Truth that comes from discovering your identity in Jesus Christ. If we aren't careful, we can choose to be religious more than relational with God. Being relational with God is an intentional journey to come to fully understand and live in your identity in Him. We need the Holy Spirit's help, the Truth of Scripture, skilled helpers and counselors, Spirit-filled pastors and teachers, and honest people in our lives. Through these sources, His Truth anchors us. It will keep us from being driven and tossed by the wind and waves of the subjective opinions and feelings of others and ourselves. This process happens in community with God and His children.

Evaluate where you are choosing to put your energy and efforts. When you think that no one else can do what you do, you confuse the lie that says you are irreplaceable with the truth that no one else is uniquely you. The purpose of life isn't to be irreplaceable; it is to be in a relationship with God that is indestructible. When I had to step away from being a local church pastor, it was stunning how fast everyone moved on. Most of what I had been doing to spin the plates of "keeping things going" stopped. The funny thing is the world didn't stop nor did the people in it. It was painful, but ultimately it was a good pain. It forced me to evaluate who and what I was called to be and to reevaluate the best uses of my time and energies.

My calling to ministry remained strong and became more resolute, but I had to learn that many of the tasks I used to do in ministry were not effective or healthy. I believe many identify with this because they try to do too much as well. The motives on why we do this vary because each person is unique. Our stories are different. What is the same is the need to sift and sort how life is being invested. If we are overtasking ourselves and others and making life revolve around this obsessive pursuit, life gets cluttered, confusing, and crisis driven.

Forgive others and yourself. One writer said it this way, "The person who can't forgive is destroying the bridge that he himself

121

must one day cross." In our desire for someone else to not "get away with it," and get some personal sense of justice, we end up being controlled by their sin and failure. Whether it reveals itself through a bitter heart or a blinded life, an unforgiving spirit destroys the one who is gripped by it.

God, the Father, has declared victory on your behalf through His Son Jesus Christ, in the power of His Holy Spirit. The greatest victory you can ever experience has already been accomplished by the infinite love of God on your behalf. It is amazing! We get to reap the benefits of a victory we did nothing to achieve.

Imagine a Gold Medalist Olympic athlete sharing their medal with you and declaring you a victor alongside him. Wouldn't it be odd to stand on the podium and receive the reward along with them for a victory that was not yours? As ludicrous as that sounds, this is what your Father has done for you. Jesus Christ won the victory, and we get the blessings. He gives us forgiveness from sins, identity as His sons and daughters, the supernatural indwelling of His Holy Spirit, the living Truth of the Holy Scriptures, His supernatural power for living, and His grace that carries us from salvation all the way to eternity in heaven.

Choose a life that isn't too small in its scope. Many of the victories we seek in this life really don't matter that much in the grand scheme of things. A couple of years ago I sat and listened to Kevin Malone, the former general manager of the Los Angeles Dodgers, share about a documentary that was produced to tell part of his family's story. He shared that for years his life was too small because it missed what God said was big–his family and his son. The gripping documentary *Shawn* reveals how life fell apart in the pursuit of accolades that were ultimately small in the grand scheme of things. Although I consider myself to be a sports "buff," I don't remember hearing about Kevin since he left his role in the major leagues. Once he was finished in that job, someone else took over, and the machine of the organization moved forward. However, the life he and his wife are living now is impacting far more than ever before. When our life is small in regard to the things God considers important, life will become small, no matter how "big" it seems to be to others.

Jesus loves you, period. You can't do anything to get Him to love you more than He already does, and you can't do anything for Him to love you any less. It may not be original, but how would life be different if we really believed it? Tim Timmons is a great songwriter, singer, and worship leader. He led the singing at a retreat my wife and I attended. During the worship-song set, he would stop singing the lyrics of the song but keep playing the guitar, but it wasn't a bridge or an instrumental solo. Instead, he would sing questions to us on how life would be different if we really lived like we believed what we were just singing. It wasn't condemning or degrading, but rather life-giving. Over the three days at this retreat, Barb and I experienced joy and peace, release and relief. It came from celebrating Truths we knew but needed to embrace again. Tim's song, "What If I Believed," has become one of our favorites on Spotify.

***

He is The Winner! Victory is Mine! This isn't some self-absorbed declaration or taking credit where we don't deserve it. It is a confession that victory comes when God's transforming power changes us. He defines and declares victory for us. He offers the same promises for each one of us if we will surrender ourselves to Him and let Him give us the victory He already fought for and won on our behalf. This life does have losses and pain, but it isn't the end of the story, or at least it doesn't have to be. We can cry out, *"He is the winner! Victory is mine!"*

ABOUT THE AUTHOR

Kevin and Barbara can be reached at ***befortified.life*** if you would like to connect with them further or ask about having them come speak to your group/church/event.

ABOUT KHARIS PUBLISHING

Kharis Publishing is a faith and inspirational publisher with a core mission to publish impactful books, and channel proceeds into establishing mini-libraries or resource centers for orphanages in developing countries, so these kids will learn to read, dream, and grow. Every time you purchase a book from Kharis Publishing or partner as an author, you are helping give these kids an amazing opportunity to read, dream, and grow. Kharis Publishing is an imprint of Kharis Media LLC. Learn more at www.kharispublishing.com.

CPSIA information can be obtained
at www.ICGtesting.com
Printed in the USA
FFHW010834151119
56056357-62035FF

9 781946 277480